Crafting a Meaningful Home

Crafting a
Meaningful Home

27 *DIY* Projects to Tell Stories, Hold Memories,
and Celebrate Family Heritage

Meg Mateo Ilasco

Photographs by Thayer Allyson Gowdy

STC Craft | A Melanie Falick Book | Stewart, Tabori & Chang | New York

Published in 2010 by Stewart, Tabori & Chang

An imprint of ABRAMS

Text and illustrations copyright © 2010 Meg Mateo Ilasco

Photographs copyright © 2010 Thayer Allyson Gowdy

Library of Congress Cataloging-in-Publication Data:

Ilasco, Meg Mateo.
  Crafting a meaningful home / Meg Mateo Ilasco ; photographs by Thayer Allyson Gowdy.
    p. cm.
  Includes bibliographical references.
  ISBN 978-1-58479-867-5
  1. Handicraft. 2. Decoration and ornament. I. Title.
  TT857.I43 2010
  745.5--dc22

                    2009047341

Editor: Melanie Falick
Designer: Meg Mateo Ilasco
Production Manager: Jacqueline Poirier

The text of this book was composed in Affair, Bodoni Egyptian, Mrs Eaves, and Gotham.

Printed and bound in China
10 9 8 7 6 5 4 3 2 1

Stewart, Tabori & Chang books are available at special discounts when purchased in quantity for premiums and promotions as well as fundraising or educational use. Special editions can also be created to specification. For details, contact specialsales@abramsbooks.com or the address below.

ABRAMS
THE ART OF BOOKS SINCE 1949

115 West 18th Street
New York, NY 10011
www.abramsbooks.com

For my mom and dad,

Alfonso and Dely Mateo

Contents

A home is many things: **a place of security**
to protect us from the elements, a place of comfort and celebration, a place for entertaining when company drops in. A home can also be an instrument for telling stories, holding memories, and sharing history and culture. The way we decorate our homes gives clues to others about who we are. As we fill them with objects that are meaningful to us, they become domestic scrapbooks that evolve over time as our lives progress.

In this book, I share stories from individuals and couples who have brought their memories, histories, and cultures into their homes through original DIY projects. Some projects pay tribute to family heritage, such as Oorbee Roy's Alpona Pillow (page 60), inspired by a type of decorative Indian painting she learned from her mother, and Diana Fayt's Folklore Chair (page 100), the cushion of which is silk-screened with Hungarian folk motifs. Some projects honor memories of loved ones, including Dad's Patchwork Coverlet by Rae Dunn (page 26). A few projects celebrate wanderlust, such as Paula Smail's Decoupaged London (page 76), a refrigerator covered with a map of London. Others honor romance, like Nick and Lisa Wong Jackson's Love Notes (page 72), an artful assembly of framed notes the two have exchanged during their years together.

All of the contributors generously shared instructions for making their projects, so that you and I can reproduce them as is or with our own adaptations to reflect our own stories. The instructions for each project are complete so that even if you've never tried a particular craft, such as silk-screening, decoupage, crochet, or gold-leafing, you will have all of the information you need to be successful.

Though each of the projects tells a different story and utilizes a different craft technique, they all celebrate the desire to make one-of-a-kind objects with personal meaning. While rooted in history, each project feels distinctly modern, thanks to the creativity and fresh perspectives of their makers.

Without a doubt, it's fun to look at homes that are tricked out with uberhip furnishings or painstakingly painted in the perfect palette, but the homes I find most interesting and comfortable—the ones that really resonate with me—are the ones that reveal stories about the people who live in them. If you agree with me, then I'm sure you will be as inspired by the projects in this book as I am.

Welcome!

Meg

Projects

Folk Art Replica

marvin & meg mateo ilasco
pinole, california

When my husband, Marvin, and I moved into

our home in Pinole, California, we decided to use our new living space as a
canvas on which to tell our stories and express our interests, personalities, and
style. We scoured estate sales and thrift stores to find the mid-century modern
Scandinavian furniture we both love. We created a wall of family photographs
in our living room and displayed our toddler daughter's artwork throughout
the house. We hung vintage motorcycle prints to showcase my husband's passion for restoring old bikes, and used beakers, flasks, and a wooden molecular
model as decorative objects to represent his work in biotechnology. I chose
screen-printed posters for the family room to express my enthusiasm for
printmaking, and collected handmade home accessories from local artisans
I admired. We spent over a year collecting, arranging, and rearranging, but
when we looked around afterwards, we realized a crucial element in our story
was still missing, in some ways the most important and obvious one: that is,
our Philippine heritage. As soon as we filled in this omission, our home felt
personal and complete.

Understandably, as children of Philippine immigrants, Marvin and I both
grew up in homes filled with Philippine decorations. However, neither of us
was thrilled about it. In my teen years, I remember wishing my house could be
more like my friends' homes, which didn't seem to reflect any particular eth-
nicity. But today, Marvin and I realize that our heritage is an important part
of our story and we enjoy incorporating it into our home, albeit on our own
terms. We mix tribal pottery with contemporary ceramics. We adapt traditional
pieces to our modern sensibilities. Here, we took Philippine wooden tinikling
dancers, a traditional wall art, and recast them in plaster. So now we not only
have a replica of the originals that once resided in my parents' living room,
but we've also brought a contemporary spin to a Philippine folk art classic.

Folk Art Replica

My husband and I created a plaster replica of wooden Philippine folk art by applying liquid latex over the original art to produce a mold. It is possible to create a mold of any dimensional wall art using the latex mold technique as long as the artwork lies flat on one side.

Finished size as shown: 27 ½ x 23"

MATERIALS

Philippine tinikling wood wall art or any wood art that lies flat on a wall

1 pound plasteline

1 quart liquid latex

Ivory dishwashing soap

Plaster of paris

4 pushpin sawtooth hangers

4 screws (for wood or drywall)

TOOLS

Cloth or rag

Drop cloth

24 x 28" glass or acrylic sheet

Glue gun and glue sticks

Small dowel or skewer

Three 1 ½"-wide paintbrushes

Fan or blow dryer

Scissors

Uncooked rice

Large aluminum tray

1 cup measuring cup

1 quart mixing container

Wooden mixing stick

Trowel

Paper towels

Screwdriver

1. With water and a damp cloth, clean the surface of your wood wall art. Let dry.

2. Cover your work surface with a drop cloth. Place the glass or acrylic sheet on the work surface. Position the wall art pieces flat side down on your glass surface so that any individual pieces are at least 3" apart from each other. Using your glue gun, apply a small amount of glue to the backs of each wood piece. (If you are working with tinikling dancers, use only the dancers to create the molds; set the tinikling sticks aside.)

3. Apply small pieces of plasteline with your fingers to any gaps between the glass and perimeter of the wood wall art. The plasteline should follow the edges of the wood wall art. Trim off any excess plasteline by running a small dowel or skewer along the edges of the wood wall art.

⟫⟶

I apply plasteline to the perimeter of the wood pieces so they will be flat (Step 3), while Marvin paints a layer of latex on another piece (Step 4).

4. With your paintbrush, brush a thin, even coat of latex onto each wood piece and onto the glass surface, forming a I to 2" flange around the base of the each piece. This flange will support the mold when casting. Make sure that any air bubbles in the latex are popped. Let dry completely until the coat appears to be translucent.

5. Apply 8 to 20 coats of latex on each piece (the latex should be ⅛ to ¼" thick). Each coat should be painted in alternating directions (horizontally, vertically, and diagonally) to strengthen the mold. Allow the latex to dry fully between coats, but no more than 24 hours should pass between coats. You can speed the drying time with a fan or blow dryer. Clean your brush with dishwashing soap and warm water between coats. You will need to replace your used brush with a new one at least two times throughout the process.

6. After the last coat, let the mold cure for at least 24 hours. Peel the mold slowly off the glass and

wood art. Use scissors to separate any pieces with connecting flanges.

7. Clean the molds with water and dishwashing soap, removing pieces of plasteline that may have adhered to them. Allow to dry completely.

8. Pour rice into your aluminum tray, about 2" deep. Place one mold in the tray, pushing into the rice so that the flange is level with the rice. The rice will help support the mold once the plaster has been poured. With a small amount of Ivory dishwashing soap on your fingers, lubricate the inside of the mold. This will help release the cast plaster.

9. Using a 2-to-I ratio of plaster to cold water, mix about 2 cups of plaster in your mixing container. Stir to a smooth consistency.

10. Pour the plaster slowly into the mold, covering all areas. Use a trowel to even the top of the cast plaster. Wipe off any excess plaster on the mold immediately with a damp paper towel.

11. When the plaster has begun to harden but is still soft, push a prenailed sawtooth hanger into the middle of your cast piece. Allow the plaster to cure per the package instructions.

12. Slowly remove your cast from the mold. Clean the mold with water and dishwashing soap.

13. Repeat steps 8 through 12 for the remaining molds.

14. After the last casting, allow the pieces to cure 24 hours before hanging them on the wall.

15. Position your finished pieces on the wall to determine where to place the screws. Insert the screws into the wall and hang the pieces. Lastly, if you made tinikling dancers, insert the small wooden tinikling sticks into the holes (set by the mold) in the bottom two dancers. Make sure the sticks are crossed.

I slowly peel the latex mold off the wood art and glass (Step 6).

Decoupaged Plates

lisa congdon
san francisco, california

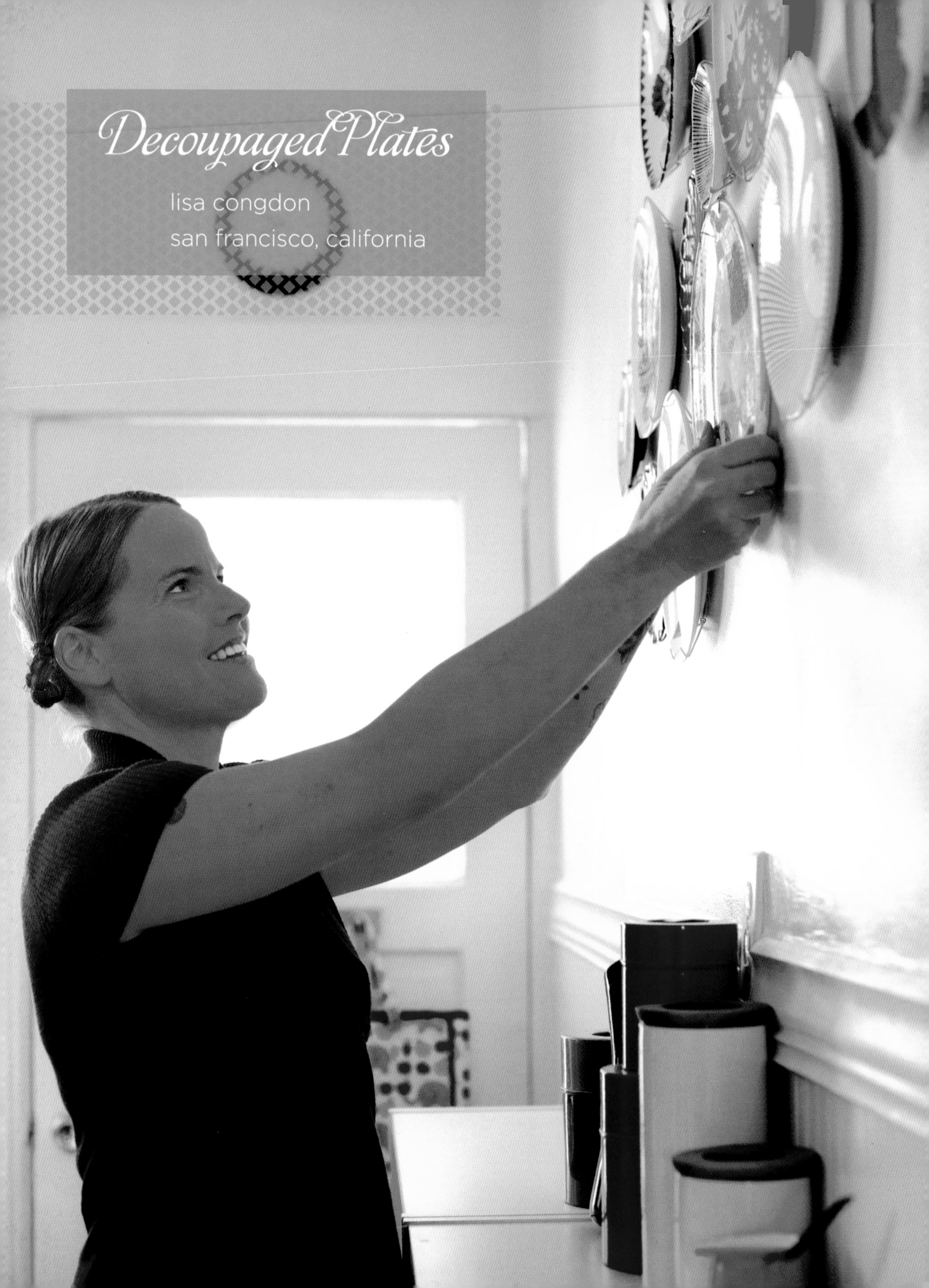

Although Lisa Congdon, her younger sister

Stephanie, and her mother Gerrie can confidently call themselves artists now, this was hardly the case four years ago. Back then, Lisa was a director in a non-profit educational organization, Stephanie, a stay-at-home mom, and Gerrie, a retired food writer. Although Gerrie had exposed her children to art while they were growing up, neither of her daughters pursued any formal training. So when Lisa decided to take a Friday-night painting class in 2001, she was surprised to discover she actually had talent. Likewise, the other Congdon women began to explore the depths of their creativity, Stephanie with sewing stuffed animals and Gerrie with art quilting.

With their latent talents coming to the surface, Lisa, Stephanie, and Gerrie began blogging to share the things they were making. It was especially helpful because Lisa lived in San Francisco while Gerrie was over an hour away in Santa Rosa, California, and Stephanie in Portland, Oregon. The blogs became a way to express mutual support, stir motivation, and show each other their latest experiments, like Lisa trying her hand at collage and Stephanie getting behind a camera. At the time, they weren't thinking about using their blogs to reach a larger public audience—but they did. Blogging quickly put all their work in the public eye. Lisa found herself being offered her first art show in Seattle, Stephanie received online orders, and Gerrie got commissions for quilts. As more offers followed suit, Lisa began to realize that she could make a living from her art. By 2007, she was not only a full-time artist but also a co-owner of the boutique Rare Device in San Francisco.

As a tribute to the two women with whom she had shared parallel creative journeys, Lisa decoupaged plates dedicated to her sister and mother. To capture the essence of each person, Lisa chose papers with colors expressive of their personalities and included imagery and memorabilia connected to each woman. For her mother, she made a chartreuse-based plate, which is her mother's favorite color and also a nod toward her love of nature. The images on the plate include illustrations of trees, a photo of Gerrie at five years old in upstate New York, an image of a European building (to represent travel), and replicas of Depression-era ration stamps from Gerrie's childhood. Because Stephanie has a quiet and gentle demeanor, Lisa chose pink-toned papers but included punches of orange, representative of Stephanie's energy. Lisa created a very modest plate without Stephanie's picture because, as Lisa says, "She would hate to have her picture in it." Alongside her vintage plate collection, Lisa has inserted these familial plates, which stand as a tribute to loved ones as well as to creativity.

Decoupaged Plates

Lisa Congdon decoupaged glass plates to celebrate the creative bonds she shares with her mother and sister. Made with decorative paper and photocopied memorabilia, decoupaged plates can commemorate any of the meaningful people in your life, special places you've traveled, or personal milestones.

Finished size as shown: 12" diameter

MATERIALS (for one plate)

I to 3 photographs

I or 2 pieces memorabilia, such as letters or documents

I to 3 pieces small artwork or illustrations

8 ½ x 11" paper for laser copiers

10 to 15 pieces decorative paper

8-ounce jar Mod Podge decoupage glue

8" to 12" clear glass plate without any imprint on the back side

Plate hanger

Nail

TOOLS

Laser color copier

Scissors

1"-wide paintbrush

Glass cleaner

Paper towels

Hammer

1. Using a laser color copier, photocopy any photographs, memorabilia, and personal artwork that you intend to use. Copy the images onto copier paper, not photo paper, so that the decoupage glue will bond.

2. On a large, clean work surface, cut out a variety of shapes from the decorative paper and copied photographs and memorabilia. Make sure you have a good assortment of shapes, sizes, contrasting colors, and patterns. You may need to cut additional pieces later to achieve a pleasing composition within the overall design.

3. Using a paintbrush, apply decoupage glue in long thin strokes to the area on the back of the plate where the first piece will be placed. Start with small pieces—these will be the images you see first from the front of the plate. Apply another thin layer of decoupage glue to the back of the paper after it is on the plate.

4. Once you have attached the smaller pieces, slowly work your way out with the larger images and pieces of paper.

5. Once you have covered the entire plate with paper, apply another layer of decoupage glue over the back. Let dry overnight.

6. Clean the glass on the front of the plate with glass cleaner and paper towels. Attach a plate hanger to your plate. Hammer a nail into the wall and hang the plate.

Travel A to Z

anh-minh le
san francisco, california

Getting her first passport a year before her

thirtieth birthday inspired Anh-Minh Le to make up for lost time. Though technically she had taken her first international trip at six months of age, emigrating with her family from Vietnam to the United States, it would be nearly three decades before she would cross an ocean again. Growing up, the furthest distance she traveled was by car from the Bay Area to Southern California to visit relatives. Even college and post-graduate studies—at the University of California at Santa Cruz and Berkeley, respectively—were both well within sixty miles of her home in Daly City, California. By the time Anh-Minh was in early adulthood she was restless and ready to explore the world.

Her first trip abroad in 2004 would indeed be a momentous one: her honeymoon to Europe with her husband, Jon Hallam. Unlike with Anh-Minh, travel had been a staple in Jon's life. His father had a Coast Guard captain's license, and the family often took boating trips. Jon even went backpacking around Europe after finishing undergraduate studies at Haverford College in Pennsylvania. The first stop on their honeymoon and the first place Anh-Minh visited outside of the United States was Amsterdam, followed by Bruges, both of which coincidentally start with the first two letters of the alphabet. Anh-Minh remembers marveling at how old the buildings were in those cities. It became clear to her just how young the United States is by comparison. Her first steps outside of the United States expanded her view of the world.

In her A to Z travel poster, Anh-Minh chronicles her adventures by placing photographs from her trips behind cut-out letters. Each letter represents a different location. Naturally, A and B are for Amsterdam and Bruges. Since 2004, Anh-Minh and Jon (along with friends and family members) have traveled together to many exotic locations, including London, Paris, Hong Kong, Tokyo, Italy, Moscow, Mexico, Canada, Turks and Caicos, Scotland, Bucharest, and Prague, to name a few. They have also traveled domestically—to New York, Austin, Boston, Seattle, Chicago, and Hilton Head Island, South Carolina, where Jon's parents currently reside. But, of course, Anh-Minh is anticipating more travel to come. For the letters of the places that she has yet to explore she simply leaves a solid color, serving as a placeholder for future travels. She's looking forward to filling D, J, Q, U, X, and Z, but admits the letter X will be a challenge.

Travel A to Z

Anh-Minh Le's A to Z poster serves as a visual travelogue of places she has visited. Photographs from various cities peer from behind cut-out letters. Since the letters frame a limited view, photographs with bold colors or those that are abstract in nature work best.

Finished size as shown: 22 x 28"

MATERIALS

22 x 28" poster board

26 A to Z alphabet stencils, 4" tall (available at craft stores)

Up to 26 photos (4 x 6") of cities/places, one for each letter of the alphabet

Colored paper

22 x 28" picture frame

TOOLS

Ruler

Soft lead pencil

Painter's tape or removable tape

Cutting mat

Small utility knife and replacement blades

1. On a clean, flat work surface, place your poster board face down and orient vertically.

2. On an area next to your poster board, arrange your alphabet stencils in five rows (as shown below).

A B C D E

F G H I J K

L M N O P

Q R S T U

V W X Y Z

3. Using your ruler and pencil, mark a 2" margin along the top and bottom of the poster board. Draw horizontal lines for each row every 4" with a 1" margin between rows.

4. Starting with letters A through E (row 1) tape the stencils to the poster board face down. You will be working in reverse starting with the letter E on the left-hand side and ending with A on the far right. Space the letters evenly across the guideline. Carefully trace each stencil with your pencil.

5. Repeat Step 4 for the remaining rows—letters F through K (row 2), L through P (row 3), Q through U (row 4), and V through Z (row 5).

6. Place your cutting mat underneath the poster board. With a small utility knife, slowly cut out each letter. Use your ruler with your knife to achieve straight edges. Replace the blade every 10 to 15 cuts, especially if you are using the blade's tip. For cutting curves, do not cut all the way through on the first cut. First score the curve with the blade, then run the knife along the curve. It may take two or three passes before you cut all the way through the poster board.

7. Organize your travel photos alphabetically from A to Z. Tape each photograph to the poster board face down in the corresponding letter opening. For example, a snapshot from Amsterdam would be taped over the letter A. Trim pictures, if necessary. If you do not have enough travel photos to fill all the letters, simply cut and tape a colored piece of paper as a placeholder. Flip the board over to make sure the photos are showing through the letters.

8. Place the poster board face down and secure it in your picture frame.

Dad's Patchwork Coverlet

rae dunn
emeryville, california

When a loved one dies, eventually family
members must deal with the possessions left behind. When Rae Dunn's father, Roy Dunn, passed away in 2008, she and her mother, Conchita, faced a heart-wrenching decision—hold on to his possessions or donate them to a local thrift store. For months his clothes sat in the closet because neither Rae nor her mother could bring herself to part with them.

Clothing stirs up distinct memories—through style, color, texture, scent, and even associations with times and events. Within his family, Roy Dunn was known for wearing button-down shirts. He wore some for work and others for leisure, such as when he played golf or went fishing. While looking at his shirts one day, Rae thought about her childhood in Fresno, California, when her father would return home from a long day working as a cook at his restaurant. He'd wake Rae, eat a little snack with her, and then tuck her back into bed. Rae then had an idea—she would take some of his shirts and turn them into a coverlet. After carefully cutting them into large rectangles, intentionally preserving areas with buttons or pockets, she sewed them together and applied a soft flannel backing. As a surprise, she presented the coverlet to her mother so she could literally wrap herself in memories of her husband.

Dad's Patchwork Coverlet

Rae Dunn sewed a memorial patchwork coverlet after her father passed away. She used his old shirts to make the coverlet, choosing parts of the shirts with interesting accents, such as buttons or pockets, for some of the pieces. For visual interest, Rae also alternated the orientation of the fabric, so the designs sometimes run in the opposite direction.

Finished size as shown: 62 x 63"

MATERIALS

14 woven cotton button-down shirts for coverlet front

4 yards 44"-wide flannel fabric for coverlet back

Matching sewing thread

TOOLS

Iron and ironing board

Clear acrylic grid ruler

Fabric marker

Rotary cutter

Cutting mat

Fabric scissors

Sewing pins

Sewing machine

Measuring tape

Sewing needle

1. Wash, dry, and iron all fabric before cutting.

2. On each shirt, measure and mark 16 x 11" rectangles using a clear grid ruler and fabric marker. You can vary the 16" width of the rectangles, if desired. Depending on the size of the shirt, it can yield at least two pieces, if not more. Mark at least twenty-seven rectangles to start.

3. Cut out the fabric rectangles using your rotary cutter, cutting mat, and ruler.

4. Arrange the rectangles in six horizontal rows of four to five rectangles each, staggering the pieces so the joins between rectangles are offset from row to row. Play with the composition until you find a layout that suits you, cutting additional rectangles of fabric, if necessary. Note that some rows may be longer than others and the edges may not align on the right and left sides of the layout. The excess fabric will be trimmed off later.

5. Working with the first horizontal row (row 1), pin the first two rectangles right sides together along the 11" edges.

≫⟶

6. Using your sewing machine, stitch along the pinned edges using a ¼" seam allowance and backstitching at the ends.

7. Continue joining the remaining row I rectangles in the same manner as for the first pair, until all the rectangles are joined end to end to complete the row. Repeat for rows 2-6.

8. Using an iron on the back side, press all seam allowances for each row to one side. On the right side, sew a zigzag stitch down the center of each seam.

9. Arrange the rows as desired, offsetting the seams from row to row. Trim off any excess fabric at the ends of the rows.

10. Pin the bottom of row I to the top of row 2, right sides together, along the length of the row.

Stitch a ¼" seam allowance along the pinned edges, backstitching at the ends. Join the remaining rows to the first two rows in the same manner, until all rows are stitched together.

11. On the back side, press all seam allowances to one side. On the right side, sew a zigzag stitch down the center of each seam.

12. If necessary, trim the right and left edges of the patchwork coverlet top, so they are straight and perpendicular to the top and bottom edges.

13. Cut the flannel backing fabric in half across the width of the fabric. Pin the two pieces of fabric, right sides together, along one long side. Stitch a ¼" seam allowance along the pinned edges, backstitching at the ends. Press the seam allowances open.

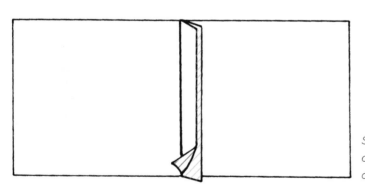

Step 8: Press seam allowances to one side on the back side of the coverlet.

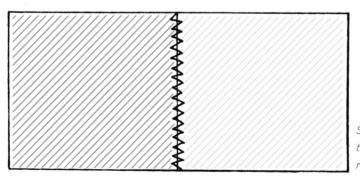

Step 8: Sew a zigzag stitch down the center of the seam on the right side of the coverlet.

Close-up of Rae's coverlet showing the zigzag stitch on the seams and on the outer edges.

14. Measure the length and width of the coverlet top. Cut a rectangle to the measured dimensions from the backing fabric. Pin the coverlet top to the backing, right sides together. Stitch ¼" from the raw edges on all sides, leaving a 12" opening on one side for turning.

15. Turn the coverlet right side out through the opening. Press the opening fabric ¼" to the wrong side and hand stitch the opening closed.

16. Zigzag stitch around the outer edges of the coverlet.

Gold-Leafed Lamp

joy deangdeelert cho
philadelphia, pennsylvania

Foil-stamped gold and metallic accents

embellish Joy Deangdeelert Cho's "Oh Joy!" stationery line, but she didn't always have such an affinity for metallics, especially gold. Growing up in a Thai family in Philadelphia, gold was ubiquitous. They had wooden chairs with gold legs, silk clothing woven with accents of gold, and artwork and photographs housed in gold frames. Joy often received gifts of gold jewelry from her relatives. As a child and teenager, she had little appreciation for this precious metal. In fact, Joy thought Thai gold—a bold, bright yellow metal with a matte finish—was just plain tacky. But during a 1999 trip to Thailand with a friend, she saw the metal from an adult perspective and began to value its beauty.

Gold is an important element in Thai culture and the act of gold-leafing has special significance. At Thai Buddhist temples and shrines, small booklets of gold leaf are often set out alongside incense, flowers, and candles, and, as an act of respect, visitors apply a square of gold leaf to a sculpture of Buddha or other sacred object. Often, so many layers of gold leaf are added that the fine details of the sculpture are obscured.

Joy has reinterpreted this tradition in her stationery line and also in her home by gold-leafing everything from lamps to vintage bottles, creating a style that reflects both Thai culture and her unique, modern sensibilities. In essence, Joy has created a personal style that is time-honored and new at the same time.

33

Gold-Leafed Lamp

Joy Deangdeelert Cho connects with her Thai culture by gold-leafing a variety of home accessories, including the lamp shown here. Amazingly, gold leaf can be applied to practically any surface.

Finished size as shown:
8 x 14" lamp base

MATERIALS

Glass lamp base

2-ounce jar gold-leaf adhesive size

Wax paper

3 or 4 sheets 5 x 5" gold leaf (also called metal leaf)

8-ounce jar gold-leaf satin-finish sealer

TOOLS

All-purpose cleaner

Two ½"-wide, flat-tipped paintbrushes

Scissors

Note: Gold-leafing kits, which include metal leaf, sealer, and adhesive size, can be purchased at most craft stores.

1. Remove the lamp shade from your lamp. Thoroughly clean the surface of your lamp base with an all-purpose cleaner.

2. Place your lamp base on your work surface. With your flat-tipped brush, apply the adhesive size to the area on the lamp where you want to apply the gold leaf. Allow to dry for at least 1 hour and up to 24 hours. When ready, the adhesive should be tacky but not wet.

3. Using scissors, cut four pieces of wax paper to 5 x 10" and fold in half (waxy side facing in) to make a 5 x 5" square. Open the wax paper and place one half, waxy side down, on top of a sheet of gold leaf. Press the wax paper against the gold leaf, applying repeated pressure with your fingers to get the leaf to stick temporarily to the wax paper. Lift the wax paper and fold the other half so that the leaf is sandwiched in between. This will allow you to cut the leaf with ease.

4. Cut the leaf into approximately 1" squares.

5. Holding one square, peel off one side of the wax paper. Starting at the top of the area covered with adhesive size, place the gold leaf on the surface and remove the wax paper. Use a dry flat-tipped paintbrush to smooth down the foil and secure it to the surface. Repeat the process, overlapping areas slightly, until the desired area is completely covered.

6. With a clean flat-tipped paintbrush, apply the sealer over the entire leafed area. Allow to dry for at least 24 hours.

7. Reattach the lamp shade to your lamp.

Vintage Fabric Display

cathy callahan
los angeles, california

Nostalgia comes in different forms. For Cathy

Callahan, it came in bolts of fabric, notions, scissors, and a sewing machine that belonged to her mother, Fran Callahan. Cathy's family lived the prototypic 1960s suburban life in San Diego. As many women of her generation had done, Fran learned to sew and make what Cathy refers to as "beautiful ladylike crafts." Though Fran was trained as a nurse, when Cathy (her only child) was born, she settled into her new role as full-time mother and housewife. After purchasing her first sewing machine, Fran sewed all of her and Cathy's clothes—a passion that allowed her to express her creativity and also stretch the family's finances. She used her machine for more than forty years, even as store-bought clothing became more affordable, until her repairman went out of business in the 1990s.

When Fran's health began to decline in 2000, she had to give up sewing. Eventually, the relentless progression of Alzheimer's even caused Fran to unknowingly throw away some of her cherished vintage sewing supplies. For safekeeping, Cathy transferred what was left to her own home. When her mother passed away, Cathy had to figure out what to do with the rest of Fran's possessions. During that process, she came to realize that a pair of scissors was more important to her than a crystal vase, and bolts of fabric more precious than china.

Cathy stored her mother's treasure trove of sewing supplies (some dating back to the 1940s) in a closet, occasionally taking a peek at them, until one day she figured out how to use the fabric. She would create a beautiful wall panel she could look at every day to honor and remember her beloved mother and her passion for sewing.

Vintage Fabric Display

Cathy Callahan mounted her mother's vintage fabrics on rectangular pieces of Gator board to create this wall art composition. You can cut the board to any shape to modify the project. Substituting fabric left over from sewing projects or from old clothes, linens, or blankets can add another layer of meaning.

Finished size as shown: 28 x 34"

MATERIALS

15 to 20 scraps vintage medium-weight cottons in various sizes

Two or three 32 x 40" pieces ½"-thick white Gator board

2 small screw eyes

No. 2 braided picture wire

10 to 20-lb. frame hanger and nail

TOOLS

Iron and ironing board

Pencil

Clear acrylic grid ruler

Cutting mat

Utility knife

Rotary cutter

Staple gun and staples

Heavy-duty T-pins, size 24

Glue gun and glue sticks

Measuring tape

Wire cutters

Hammer

1. Wash, dry, and press all fabric.

2. Using a pencil and ruler, outline fifteen to twenty squares and rectangles in a variety of sizes on your Gator board. Lay the Gator board on top of the cutting mat. Using your utility knife and ruler, carefully cut out the shapes.

3. Match your scrap fabric to the cut pieces of Gator board. Wrap the fabric around each piece of Gator board, making sure there is enough fabric to wrap around to the back of the board. Trim your Gator board if necessary. If you have too much excess fabric at the back of your board, trim your fabric to size using your rotary cutter

and ruler. Make sure the right side of the fabric is centered and lies flat against the board. Smooth out any irregularities with your hand. Use the staple gun to secure the fabric to the back of the board at each corner.

4. Create a composition with the fabric-covered boards. Play around with layering, patterns, color, and texture. Once you find a design that is visually pleasing, pin the boards together one at a time with the T-pins.

5. Starting with the top layer of boards, carefully remove the pins, working on one piece at a time. Using your glue gun, glue each board into place. As you work your way to the bottom layer, it may be helpful to carefully flip the shapes over, front sides down, and continue to glue. Let dry.

6. With the wrong side of the display facing up, use your measuring tape to determine the center of your display. Draw a horizontal line across the center with a pencil. Along this line, measure and mark 6" to 8" from each edge of the display. The distance should be equal on both sides. On each mark, turn the small screw eye in slowly by hand, making sure not to elongate the screw holes. The bottom of the screw eye's circular opening should just touch the surface of the Gator board.

7. Thread one end of the braided picture wire through one screw eye. Leave enough slack in the wire so that when it is pulled taut up against the back of the display the center point of the wire reaches about halfway between the screw eyes and the top of the display. Leave about 3" of extra wire at each end. Wrap both ends of the extra wire tightly around the hanging wire. Trim excess wire with the wire cutters.

8. Install the picture hook on the wall using the hammer and a nail. Hang the fabric wall display.

Rockite Bottle Vases

anna corpron & sean auyeung
new york, new york

Of all the design disciplines, only architecture

school qualifies as creative boot camp. Busy is an understatement. Sleep deprivation is typical. The paths that brought Anna Corpron and Sean Auyeung to this experience were very different. Born in Seattle, Washington, Anna spent her early years in Thailand and then attended a boarding school in the foothills of the Himalayas in India. Sean, on the other hand, grew up in the sleepy New England town of Windsor, Connecticut. So when Anna and Sean arrived at Cornell University in 1998, they were both somewhat ignorant of what lay ahead.

Indeed, initiation was harsh. Neither of them had anticipated the never-ending stream of assignments coupled with overwhelming fatigue nor realized that students could actually sleep in the small spaces beneath their desks. Anna fondly remembers Sean as "the talented kid who would sleep with his eyes open in class." Anna and Sean consider themselves lucky that they not only endured but also enjoyed the process. Because they were consumed with the rigors of school, it's not surprising that their romantic relationship didn't blossom until after they had both graduated and could finally rest.

After pursuing architecture jobs for several years, Anna and Sean opened a design studio called Sub-Studio Design in 2006 and married in 2007. Their experiences in architecture school still influence the products they develop for their company, like the Rockite bottle vases featured here. During the countless hours they spent building models in college, they were able to explore a variety of different materials and methods; one, in particular, was casting using Rockite, expansion cement that can be purchased at ordinary hardware stores. They began to notice that there would inevitably be leftover casting material that needed a home. Because they spent so many long nights in the studio, their work tables were always full of empty beverage bottles and coffee cups, so these containers became easy receptacles for the leftover Rockite.

As any artist knows, accidents often produce design epiphanies, and peeling off the mundane containers often yielded a beautiful form. Since then, they've refined their technique, turning plastic beverage bottle forms into functional vases. These Rockite bottle vases now sit in their home, a beautiful reminder of their experience together in architecture school.

Rockite Bottle Vases

Drawing upon the mold-making techniques they learned during architecture school, Anna Corpron and Sean Auyeung cast vases with Rockite and plastic beverage bottles. The best bottles for this project are those with interesting shapes or patterns. The bottles shown here were found at an Asian grocery store.

Finished sizes as shown: 6 x 2 ½"

MATERIALS (for one vase)

½ liter plastic beverage bottle with a pleasing shape or pattern

25 x 100mm glass test tube with a rim

Rockite (available at hardware stores)

Spray sealant with UV protection (available at hardware stores)

TOOLS

Ruler

Permanent marker

Small utility knife

Wooden dowel, 1" wide (or slightly wider than the body of the test tube)

Drop cloth

Duct tape

Paper towels

Petroleum jelly

Small bucket

Wooden mixing stick or putty knife

Bucket lid or small piece of scrap wood

Dishwashing gloves

100-grit sandpaper

1. Empty the beverage from the bottle. Clean and rinse the bottle. Let dry.

2. Measure the length of the glass test tube. The vase needs to be at least ¾" taller than the height of the test tube so that the test tube will be hidden within the vase. When you've determined how much of the bottle you would like to use to create your vase's final form, mark this height around the bottle with a permanent marker. Using your utility knife, cut off the top of the bottle to this mark.

3. Add ¼" to the height of the glass test tube and mark this height on your wooden dowel.

4. Cover your work surface with a drop cloth. Place your bottle upright on your work surface, and place the dowel inside the center of the bottle. Lift up the dowel so that the mark on the dowel lines up with the top of the bottle. Fill the bottle with water to the top. Remove the dowel from the bottle and mark the top of the water line on the outside of the bottle. Label this line "Rockite fill line." Discard the water.

⟫⟶

Sean slowly pours the Rockite while Anna holds the bottle (Step 8).

5. After your dowel has dried completely, wrap duct tape around the dowel as though you were wrapping athletic tape around the handle of a tennis racket. Apply tape to the surface to be submerged in Rockite, at least 1" past the mark on the dowel. This will keep your dowel from bonding with the Rockite. Remark the dowel on the surface of the duct tape, referring to Step 3 if necessary.

6. To aid with removal later on, use a paper towel to apply a thin layer of petroleum jelly to the tape on the dowel. Set the dowel aside.

7. Following the directions given by the manufacturer, prepare your Rockite mixture with water in a bucket. Once you've blended it together thoroughly using your mixing stick, the mixture should have the consistency of pancake batter.

8. Place the bottle on a bucket lid or scrap piece of wood on your work surface to catch any excess Rockite. Carefully pour the Rockite into your bottle up to the "Rockite fill line." Be careful because the temperature will be hot. Lightly tap on the sides of the bottle to help get rid of air bubbles.

9. Insert the dowel into the center of the bottle so that the mark on the dowel lines up with the top of the bottle. Hold the dowel in this position for about 10 minutes.

10. Gently remove the dowel by turning it clockwise and pulling it upward. At this point, the Rockite has begun its transformation from liquid to solid, but is not yet completely solid. The mixture has to be solid enough so that you can remove the dowel without changing the cast shape, but not so solid that the dowel is difficult to remove.

11. After the Rockite has solidified, use your utility knife to score the plastic bottle along its length until the bottle splits open. Make light, repetitive cuts to avoid cutting into the cast. Any shallow nicks in your cast can be lightly smoothed out with your thumb. Wearing dishwashing gloves, completely remove the cast from its plastic casing and set aside.

12. Place the sandpaper on your work surface. Wearing the dishwashing gloves, take the cast vase and hold it upside down. Slowly grind the vase in a circular motion against the sandpaper to smooth the rough surface at the top of the vase. Let the vase dry for 48 hours. Do not place in direct sunlight.

13. The color of Rockite will change over time if exposed to direct sunlight. Coat the entire surface of the vase with a spray sealant to help protect it from sun and water. Let dry.

14. Insert the test tube, and your vase is complete.

Sean carefully holds the dowel in place as the Rockite transforms from liquid to solid (Step 9).

Sean scores the plastic bottle so that it can be removed from the Rockite vase (Step 11).

Memory Wall

lauren smith & derek fagerstrom
san francisco, california

As owners of The Curiosity Shoppe, a boutique

in San Francisco, Lauren Smith and Derek Fagerstrom spend many of their waking hours contemplating objects—from their shape, size, weight, and price to who made them, what they're made of, and where they come from. It's these considerations that form an object's story, and if the story resonates with them, it earns a place in their shop. This thoughtful, curatorial approach isn't limited to their shop merchandising either. They apply it in their home by carefully choosing objects that relay their interests, tastes, and stories.

With a relationship spanning more than fifteen years, they do indeed have stories to share. Lauren and Derek met during their freshman year at the University of California at Santa Cruz. Mesmerized by her beauty, Derek developed a crush on Lauren from afar. One anonymous email and one Fellini film date later, it was clear they had a lot in common—namely an interest in art and music. They went from hanging out on a daily basis to eventually moving in together by the end of their freshman year. Their partnership has always involved artistic collaboration as well. They curated their first art show together during their junior year abroad in Venice.

Their love of collaboration is apparent in the memory wall they created in their bedroom, which is composed of toys, gifts, artwork, and ephemera the couple have been collecting over the years—like an embroidery hoop that says "L+D 4 ever!" made by Lauren when she was first learning how to embroider; a ukelele symbolizing their love for music; and quirky tournament-model slingshots, which they just simply adore. A shadow box carries keys from every apartment they've shared. A drawer backed with cork affords more space to showcase memorabilia from their log cabin wedding, including a hand-printed invitation as well as patches they collected during their honeymoon to Grand Teton and Yellowstone. A six-pane vintage window backed with construction paper is fashioned into a photograph and artwork holder. A cigar box jutting out of the wall holds notes and cards they've sent to each other.

"Objects invite conversation in ways photographs do not," explains Derek. "People can make many assumptions about an image, but a slingshot on the wall or a set of keys in a box? It's literally begging for questions. It leads to a deeper level of storytelling."

Memory Wall

Lauren Smith and Derek Fagerstrom's memory wall relays the story of their courtship and marriage through special objects and images. When putting together your own memory wall, they recommend hanging objects in a variety of shapes, colors, and patterns to create a dynamic composition. They also suggest keeping flexibility in mind (like lining the drawer with corkboard or using pushpins to hold items) so that you can swap out or add objects as time goes on.

Finished overall size as shown:
50 x 36"

MATERIALS

Shadow box

2 ounces acrylic paint in color of your choice

Remnant wallpaper or decorative paper

6 keys

3 nails

Drawer

Cork roll

Spray adhesive

2 sawtooth hangers

Photographs

Personal objects that vary in shape, size, depth, material, and color

Pushpins

Old 6-pane window

Photo corners (optional)

2 medium screw eyes

2 medium cup hooks

Screws for wood or drywall (optional)

TOOLS

Newspaper

Painter's tape

½"-wide paintbrush

Measuring tape

Scissors

Double-stick tape

Hammer

Cloth or rag

All-purpose cleaner

Cutting mat

Metal ruler

Utility knife

Spray adhesive

Screwdriver (optional)

Double-stick foam tape (optional)

Putty or museum wax (optional)

Note: Lauren and Derek used a 6 ¼ x 6 ¼" shadow box, a 22 x 14 x 5" drawer, and a 22 x 33 ½" window for their memory wall.

Key Box

1. Cover your work surface with newspaper. Place your shadow box frame on your work surface. Line the edges of the glass front with painter's tape. With your paintbrush, apply paint to the frame. Let dry.

Derek and Lauren fill a vintage drawer with wedding memorabilia.

2. Measure the inside of the shadow box. On a cutting mat, use a metal ruler and a utility knife to cut a piece of decorative paper to those dimensions. Apply double-stick tape to the back of the decorative paper and press it to the inside of the shadow box.

3. Apply a thin strip of double-stick tape to one side of each key. Press them onto the decorative paper, placing the keys in rows of three.

4. Hammer a nail into the wall and hang your frame.

Memorabilia Drawer

1. On your work surface, clean the drawer with a damp cloth and all-purpose cleaner.

2. Measure the bottom of the drawer. On a cutting mat, use a metal ruler and a utility knife to trim the cork to those dimensions. Spray one side of the cork with adhesive and attach it to the drawer bottom.

3. Flip the drawer over. Attach two sawtooth hangers to the back of the drawer, about 1" from the top edge.

4. Attach photographs and ephemera to the cork using pushpins.

5. Hammer two nails into the wall and hang the drawer. Place objects such as vases or figurines inside the drawer.

Artwork and Photograph Window

1. On your work surface, wipe the window with a damp cloth and all-purpose cleaner.

2. Measure the interior of one pane. Cut six pieces of decorative paper to those dimensions.

3. Affix photo corners to pictures and place them on the decorative paper or adhere double-stick tape to the back of small pieces of artwork and place them on the decorative paper.

4. Place double-stick tape on the front side of each decorative paper. Attach one paper to the back side of each pane of glass.

5. Screw two screw eyes into the top of the window frame. Screw two cup hooks into the wall. Slip the screw eyes over the hooks and hang the window on the wall.

Other Objects

Other objects and memorabilia can be hung on the wall using screws or double-stick foam tape. If you plan to change your memory wall often, you can use putty or museum wax to adhere light-weight objects to it.

Letters and notes are stored in a cigar box that also serves as a shelf to display cards.

Silhouettes on Canvas

haile mccollum
thomasville, georgia

When adults decide they are ready to start a family, they sometimes feel their hometown beckoning their return. After living in Jackson, Wyoming, for several years, Haile, a graphic designer, and her then boyfriend Ben McCollum, who owned a real estate brokerage, decided that Thomasville, Georgia, would be the ideal place to settle. Indeed, five generations of Haile and Ben's families have lived there—Thomasville is practically in their DNA.

On a serendipitous drive through Thomasville in March 2005, Haile and Ben came across a For Sale sign on a home they knew well: the David Harell House. Built in 1853, the grand property had tragically fallen into disrepair. But in their eyes, it was a perfect fit for them—Ben loved the idea of restoring an historic property and Haile desired a large home in which to continue the tradition of gracious hosting for which her family was known.

Bringing her Southern family heritage into her home is something that is second nature for Haile. After her parents passed away when she was 23, she became the unspoken family-appointed genealogist and repository for heirloom odds and ends, including her mother's collection of brass oil lamps, her grandfather's slide rule, and framed silhouettes of ancestors. Inspired by these silhouettes, including one of Dr. Thomas Walker, an explorer (circa mid-1700s), and her grandmother, Judith Maury Tice (circa early 1900s), Haile made profile portraits of her sons, Parker and William, when each was 20 months old, and even one of their dog, Amos.

When it comes to restoring and decorating an historic property, Haile understands the need to strike a balance between maintaining the home's original character and imagining and creating something new and relevant. To that end, she has struck a happy medium by including traditional family silhouettes in modern arrangements throughout her home. Though the past serves as her inspiration, the result feels contemporary.

ʃilhouettes on Canvas

Carrying on her family tradition of silhouette portraits, Haile McCollum traced and cut her children's profiles from black paper and adhered them to painted oval canvases. Adding a bit of humor, Haile also silhouetted the family dog.

ished sizes as shown: 8 x 10"

MATERIALS (for one silhouette)

8 x 10" oval stretched canvas

2 ounces acrylic paint in color of your choice (turquoise was used here)

8 ½ x 11" sheet white medium-weight paper

8 ½ x 11" sheet black heavyweight paper

Mod Podge decoupage glue

Picture hanging strip

TOOLS

Drop cloth

1"-wide paintbrush

Digital camera

Computer and printer

Fine-tip scissors

Tape

1. Cover your work surface with a drop cloth. Place the canvas on the cloth.

2. Using the acrylic paint and quick, even strokes, paint the canvas and let dry.

3. With a digital camera, take a profile photo of a family member. To do this, have the person stand against a white wall, and include only his or her profile (head to shoulders) in each shot. Upload the photos onto a computer and resize if necessary.

4. Print out the photo onto medium-weight paper and carefully cut out the profile with fine-tip scissors. Be sure to get every detail, such as bangs, ponytails, or any little pieces of hair sticking up. Once you have cut around all the edges, secure the cutout to the black paper with tape and, using the cutout as a template, cut the black paper to match.

5. Brush the decoupage glue onto the back of the profile and carefully center it on the canvas. Let dry. Apply another thin layer of decoupage glue over the entire canvas.

6. To hang, attach the adhesive on the picture hanging strip to the back of the canvas and stick to the wall.

Braided Rag Vessels

sian keegan
brooklyn, new york

FOR
LIKE
EVER

Sian Keegan comes from a lineage of women

inspired by the craft movements of different generations. Her maternal grandmother, Ruth Stewart, experienced the tail end of the Arts and Crafts movement. Her mother, Patricia Keegan, has the requisite macramé planter as proof of her skill during the 1970s craft revival. And Sian, a freelance textile designer with an eponymous company that creates stuffed animals, is a product of the current generation's renewed interest in the handmade. All of them experimented with various sewing and fiber crafts, but a more specific thread prevails: an interest in braided rag.

All three women hail from southern Connecticut, where braided rag rugs have had a long history. Made from scraps of fabric and requiring little sewing skill, rag rugs allowed many working-class families in the 1800s to warm and decorate their floors. Later, during the Arts and Crafts movement, there was a renewed interest in braided rag rugs with an emphasis on craft rather than thrift, and designs and techniques became more elaborate, including dyeing fabrics to create specific patterns. Because of the proximity of woolen mills in New England, many early rugs produced there, including those created by Ruth, were wool. Sian notes that her grandmother displays braided rag rugs, seat covers, and table runners throughout her home. Patricia was reintroduced to braided rag through a historical crafts class she took while pursuing her master's degree in education. She fashions her rugs out of remnant fabric, old clothes, and bed sheets in bright colors. Putting a contemporary spin on this classic, Sian makes three-dimensional braided rag vessels to hold items such as keys, knitting needles, or flowers. Oftentimes, she makes these vessels out of fabrics from her mother's and grandmother's stashes, connecting her work to the previous generations.

Braided Rag Vessels

Sian Keegan broadened her family's braided-rug tradition when she came up with this technique for forming braided fabric into vessels. The instructions here are for a 6 x 3" vessel (like the soft blue one shown in the photos at right and left), but you can create different shapes by widening the base and/or increasing the height.

Finished sizes as shown: 9 ½ x 4", 5 x 5", and 6 x 3"

MATERIALS (for one 6 x 3" vessel)

Scrap fabric (such as old clothing, sheets, leftover pieces from other projects, etc.)

Matching sewing thread

TOOLS

Measuring tape

2 safety pins

Scissors

Hand-sewing needle

Straight pins

1. Tear fabric into three strips, 2" wide x 36" long. Tie the three strips together into a knot at one end.

2. Braid the strips together. The final braid will need to be about 10' long, but it is best to work in 36" segments. Sew additional strips to the ends of braided strips as you go until you achieve the total length.

3. Undo the knot and braid the remainder of strips at that end. Attach a safety pin securely to either end of the 10' braid. With scissors, trim each end at an angle. Using your needle and thread, sew each end of the braid to secure it and remove the safety pins.

4. On a work surface, lay the braid flat. Take one end of the braid and coil the braid around itself in a circular motion to create the base of your container. Create a 3" base. Pin each row of the coil into place.

5. Using your needle and thread, make small stitches between the braided rows of the coil to secure. Remove the pins when complete.

6. When the base is secure, you will start building the vessel upward. Holding the excess braid so the flat side is facing out and is uniformly flush, coil the braid on top of the base, pinning each row in place as you coil.

7. Using a needle and thread, stitch between each row. Remove the pins when complete.

8. Tuck the end of the braid into the vessel, making sure the top of the vessel is flat, and sew in place.

Alpona Pillow

oorbee roy
toronto, canada

When Oorbee Roy and her husband Sanjeev

Shah moved into a new home in Toronto, Canada, in 2007, Oorbee decided
to decorate it in a style that melded their Indian heritage with her contemporary sensibilities and artistic flair. Oorbee is a self-taught artist with a particular fascination for Indian folk art, especially a type of painting called alpona.
Traditional alpona is ephemeral—Indian women paint floors and entryways
with geometric patterns and floral designs using an impermanent mixture of
rice flour, water, and dye for religious occasions and festivals—but in Oorbee's
house it is permanent. Her delicately formed sweeps and flourishes adorn
walls, ceilings, and pillows.

A child of Indian immigrants, Oorbee was born in Hindsdale, Illinois,
but raised in Scotch Plains, New Jersey. Oorbee learned alpona when she was
twelve from her mother, Bithi Roy, as they traced patterns in the sand along
the New Jersey shore. Because her upbringing merged American and Indian cultures, it's no surprise that over time Oorbee's alpona style became a
combination of both Western and Eastern influences. She calls her alpona a
reflection of what she "feels in her heart" more than an adherence to any strict
tradition.

Oorbee's interest in alpona heightened after a trip to Kolkata, India, in
2002, during which she met with alpona artisans and sadly found out that
their numbers were dwindling. Intent on doing her part to keep this rich art
form alive, not long after returning home Oorbee started OM Home, a company that creates textiles, such as bedding, pillows, and tablecloths, featuring
alpona patterns. Although Oorbee typically draws her alpona designs freehand, for the project presented here, she has provided a stencil, so that all of
us can easily enjoy the beauty of alpona.

Alpona Pillow

Oorbee Roy introduces us to alpona, a hand-painted Indian folk art, through a stencil pattern she created. The stenciled pattern can be applied to a variety of surfaces. But here, it is applied to fabric and sewn into a pillow.

Finished size as shown: 16 x 16"

MATERIALS

11 x 17" paper

18 x 24" sheet tinted 5 mil Mylar

⅝ yard 44" or 60"-wide mid- to heavy-weight fabric

Repositionable spray adhesive

8 ounces acrylic fabric paint

Matching sewing thread

16"-square pillow form

TOOLS

Copier

Scissors

Cellophane tape

Large cutting mat

Painter's tape or removable tape

Measuring tape

Small utility knife and replacement blades

Iron and ironing board

Fabric scissors

Kraft paper

Plastic spoon

Paper plate

Paper towels

½"-wide round stencil brush

Sewing machine

Straight pins

Point turner

Create Stencil

1. Using the alpona drawing on page 152 or your own artwork, enlarge the image on a copier by 300% (until it is 17 x 17" and fits on two sheets of 11 x 17" paper). Line up the drawings (trimming, if necessary) and tape the pieces together with cellophane tape. Allowing for a 1" margin around the assembled artwork, measure and trim the paper to 18 x 18".

2. On your work surface, place the alpona drawing, artwork-side up, on the cutting mat. Tape the corners of the drawing to the mat with painter's tape.

3. With scissors, trim the Mylar sheet to 18 x 18". Place the Mylar on top of the drawing. Tape the corners of the Mylar sheet to the mat with painter's tape.

4. With a small utility knife, cut slowly and carefully along the edges of the design. When cutting curves, do not cut all the way through on the first cut. Score the curve first with the blade. It may take two or three passes before you cut all the way through the Mylar. Replace the blade every 10 to 15 cuts, especially if you are using the blade's tip. Discard the cutout shapes from the Mylar. The remaining design on the Mylar will be your stencil. Set aside.

⟫⟶

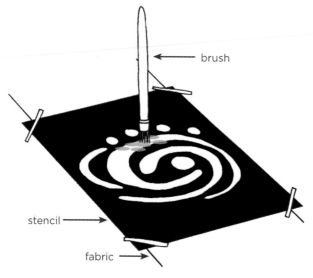

brush

stencil

fabric

Step 8: Holding your brush perpendicular to the stencil, apply paint to the fabric by stippling, or tapping the surface repeatedly to create dots of color.

Step 8: When you have finished stippling the entire design, lift your stencil to reveal the design underneath.

Stencil Fabric

5. Wash, dry, and iron your fabric before cutting. With your fabric scissors, trim your fabric to 36 x 17".

6. Cover your work surface with kraft paper. Spray adhesive on the back side of the stencil. Place the fabric, right side up, on your work surface, taping the corners down using painter's tape. Center the stencil, adhesive side down, on the fabric.

7. With a plastic spoon, scoop about a tablespoon of paint onto the paper plate. Fold a paper towel twice into fourths. Load paint onto your brush by dipping the bristles into the paint on the plate; then remove the excess paint by dabbing the brush repeatedly on the paper towel. It is important to load the brush with just the right amount of paint. Too much paint will cause paint to seep under your stencil and give your design imperfect edges.

8. Holding the brush perpendicular to the stencil, apply paint by tapping the surface repeatedly to create dots of color (a process called stippling). Stippling allows you to transfer your pattern to the fabric without getting paint under the stencil's edges. Stipple layers of paint onto the fabric until the pattern is evenly painted, reloading the brush with paint as needed. You may want to practice on excess fabric scraps first to see how much paint to put on the brush and how many layers of paint to apply. Once you have covered the entire design, slowly lift the stencil from the fabric. Wipe off any excess paint on the Mylar stencil with a paper towel. Wash your stencil brush thoroughly with water. Let the fabric dry completely.

9. Repeat the stenciling process on the remaining ends of the fabric, allowing the stencil to extend beyond the short edges of the fabric. Clean your stencil with a paper towel and wash your stencil brush thoroughly with water. Once the fabric is dry, iron it on high heat to set the paint.

Sew Pillow

10. Turn and press each short end of the stenciled fabric ¼" to the wrong side, and then turn this edge ½" to the wrong side. Using your sewing machine, stitch along the inner fold, backstitching at the ends to hem the short ends of the fabric.

11. With the right side of the fabric positioned horizontally and face up, fold the short ends toward the center overlapping them until the width of the folded fabric is 16". Aligning the top and bottom edges, pin and sew them together with a ½" seam allowance. Clip the corners.

12. Turn the pillow cover right side out. Using a point turner, push the corners out and then press. Insert the pillow form into the center opening.

Step 10: Stitch hems at the short ends of your fabric.

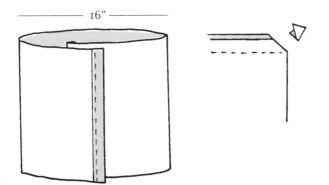

Step 11: Fold the short ends of the fabric toward the center, overlapping them until the width of the folded fabric is 16". After you've stitched the top and bottom edges of the pillow, clip the corners.

Doily Rug

jean lee

seattle, washington

All children love summers and holidays when

they are out of school, but Jean Lee and her older sister, Yilin, probably appreciated them more than most. This is because—from grade school through college—these were the only times they spent in Taiwan with their mother and father. During the rest of the year they lived with their aunt and uncle in Eugene, Oregon, where their parents believed they would get a better education. Among the many happy memories that Jean has of those coveted times in Taiwan are the hours her mother, Grace Lee, spent teaching her crafts, including origami, sewing, knitting, and crochet. Jean was especially adept at crochet and had successfully completed simple lacy doilies, hats, and bags all by the time she was ten.

Although as a child Jean didn't regard those summertime crafts as more than a fun way to share time with her mother, today she sees a direct link between those experiences and her decision to study industrial design at University of Washington, and then to cofound her two current business ventures, Chikabird, an accessory and clothing company in Seattle, Washington, and Ladies & Gentleman, a design studio and online shop for vintage home goods. When she recently came across some old crochet pattern books while scavenging for Ladies & Gentleman, she was inspired to pick up a crochet hook again and make some doilies. At first, she crocheted them out of cotton yarn just as she did as a child, but then she was struck by the idea of experimenting with materials and scale. What would happen, she wondered, if she worked traditional crochet using only rope and her hands? She was delighted with the beautiful result and the doily's new utilitarian purpose—instead of a decorative cloth, it's a lovely rug for people to sit on in her living room.

Doily Rug

Jean Lee adapted crocheted doily techniques she learned as a child to create this, literally, handmade rope rug. Although a typical doily pattern is shown here, you can easily play around with different stitches to create your own pattern. Jean uses welting cord, but for other variations you can use nylon rope, twisted cotton rope, or Manila hemp rope. Remember to adjust the tension of your stitches based on the malleability of the rope. Stiffer rope will require looser stitches.

Finished size as shown: 4' diameter

MATERIALS

300 yards 16/32"-thick cotton piping cord

4 ounces liquid fabric glue

Stitch marker, such as a safety pin

Notes: For easier stitching and to reduce bulk, work the stitches into the top loop of previous stitches only.

Keep an even tension so stitches won't be too loose or too tight. Each stitch should be loose enough for at least a finger or two to fit through the loop, but not so loose that stitches lose their structure and form.

Because rope is bulky to work with and you are crocheting with your fingers rather than a crochet hook, the stitches won't necessarily be created in a continuous motion. It will be necessary to use both hands. You may need to pull or push loops through stitches using both hands, and then realign loops on your thumb and index finger before continuing on.

Basic Crochet Stitches

1. Chain: Insert your index finger and thumb through a loop, pinch the rope and draw it through the loop to make another loop. Continue to draw one loop through each loop to make a chain of loops.

2. Single Crochet: With your thumb and index finger inserted into a loop, insert them from front to back into a chain or top loop of a stitch. Pinch and draw the rope through the chain or stitch to create a loop (A) and place the loop onto your thumb and index finger. You should have two loops over your thumb and index finger. Pinch and draw the rope through both loops (B), and then place the single loop on your thumb and index finger.

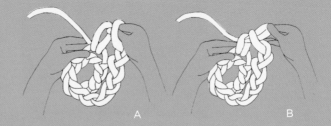

A   B

3. Double Crochet: With your thumb and index finger inserted into a loop, wrap the rope from back to front around your index finger and pinch between your thumb and index finger (A).

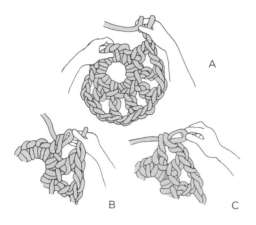

A

B

C

Insert your thumb and finger from front to back into a chain or top loop of a stitch. Wrap the rope from back to front around your index finger, pinch, and draw the rope through the chain or stitch to create a loop. Place the loops onto your

thumb and index finger. You should have three loops over your thumb and index finger. Pinch and draw the rope through two loops (B), and then place the new loop on your thumb and index finger. You should have two loops over your thumb and index finger. Pinch and draw the rope through both loops (C), and then place the single loop on your thumb and index finger.

4. Slip Stitch: With your thumb and index finger inserted into a loop, insert them from front to back into a chain or top loop of a stitch, pinch the rope and draw it through the stitch and loop on your finger, creating a new loop.

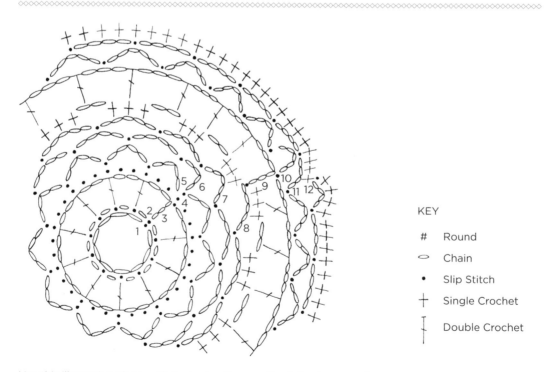

KEY

#	Round
◠	Chain
•	Slip Stitch
+	Single Crochet
⊺	Double Crochet

Use this illustration along with the instructions on the following page to create your rug.

Doily Rug Pattern

Make a circle shape about 8 to 9" from the end of the rope. Push the rope through the circle and pull the resulting loop snug to make a slip knot. Adjust the size of the loop by pulling on the rope under the knot.

Round 1: Make 10 chain stitches. Join with a slip stitch to a make a circle.

Round 2: *Slip stitch in the circle, pull the rope to the back side of the circle and chain 1. Repeat from * 10 more times.

Round 3: Make 5 chain stitches. *Skip 1 stitch, make 1 double crochet in the next stitch, and make 2 chain stitches. Repeat from * around and join with a slip stitch in the 3rd chain of the starting chain.

Starting with round 3, place a stitch marker into the last stitch of the round. At the end of the next round, move the stitch marker to the last stitch of that round.

Round 4: Slip stitch in each stitch around.

Round 5: *Make 4 chain stitches, skip 2 stitches, and make a slip stitch in the next stitch. Repeat from * around.

Round 6: *Make 4 chain stitches, then a slip stitch at the center of the chain loop made in round 5. Repeat from * around, stopping after the slip stitch at the center of the last chain loop.

Round 7: *Make 5 chain stitches, then a slip stitch at the center of the chain loop made in round 6. Repeat from * around, stopping after the slip stitch at the center of the last chain loop.

Round 8: Make 5 chain stitches, then make 3 single crochets at the center of the chain loop made in round 7. *Make 2 chain stitches, then make 3 single crochets at the center of the chain

loop made in round 7. Repeat from * around, continuing until you have made 3 single crochets at the center of the first chain loop in round 8. Join the loops with a slip stitch in the 5th, or final, chain of the starting chain.

Round 9: Make 6 chain stitches. *Skip 2 stitches, make 1 double crochet in the next stitch, and then make 3 chain stitches. Repeat from * around, skipping only 1 stitch in the last repeat, and join the loops with a slip stitch in the 3rd chain of the starting chain.

Round 10: *Make 5 chain stitches, then make a slip stitch at the center of the chain loop made in round 9. Repeat from * around, stopping after the slip stitch at the center of the last chain loop.

Round 11: *Make 4 chain stitches, then make a slip stitch at the center of the chain loop made in round 10. Repeat from * around, stopping after the slip stitch at the center of the last chain loop. Make 4 chain stitches.

Round 12: Make 3 single crochets in the next chain loop. *Single crochet in the next stitch, then make 3 single crochets in the next chain loop. Repeat from * around and join with a slip stitch in the first single crochet. Cut the rope about 6" from the last stitch and pull on the last loop to pull the end through. To prevent fraying, apply liquid glue to the end and let dry. Weave the end into the stitches on the back side of the rug.

Love Notes

nick & lisa wong jackson
berkeley, california

Being green has always been important to Lisa

Wong Jackson—from using recycled paper in her stationery line, Good on Paper, to driving an energy-efficient vehicle, to using mass transit as often as possible. Seven years ago, that commitment to mass transit paid off in an unexpected way. On her daily commute to work using BART (San Francisco Bay Area's public transit system) from the Ashby station in Berkeley to the 12th Street City Center station in Oakland, she found herself on the same schedule as an attractive stranger, Nick Jackson. After mirroring each other's morning routine repeatedly for two months, punctuated by smiles and glances from the parking lot to the train, Lisa made the first move and left a simple note on his car: "You're a cutie. Hi." Two days later, Nick returned the gesture echoing the same sentiments, "No, you're the cutie," along with his phone number and a funny disclaimer: "P.S. If this is the wrong car, please disregard."

Their first conversation lasted four hours, and it wasn't long before Nick moved into Lisa's Berkeley apartment. A couple for seven years, they've exchanged many notes, from the heartfelt to the humorous to the mundane. They each have a box containing notes they've received from each other; Lisa has hers in a red cloth-covered box, and Nick keeps his in a tin Lisa decoupaged with various dating memorabilia. However, the original notes that first brought them together are mounted in a shadow box Lisa created to display at their wedding in 2005. (Guests read their story in their invitations and saw the real notes at the reception table.) The shadow box now resides permanently on their dresser. But it occurred to Lisa and Nick—why not put the rest of their notes on display in their home? So they took some of their favorite notes and mounted them in a series of frames to make a single composition. Some of Lisa's favorite notes from Nick are "You are the sunshine of my life," a note Nick left on Valentine's Day 2006, and "Sweetie pie for sweetie pie," which accompanied a strawberry rhubarb pie Nick made from scratch for Lisa after she mentioned she'd never had rhubarb pie before. A sticky note with Lisa's handwriting says, "Poops, I will call you with the number for Park Animal Hospital." Nick laughs, "Our nickname for each other sometimes is Poops."

Love Notes

Nick and Lisa Wong Jackson celebrated their love by framing their private notes and assembling them into a wall composition. The same idea can be used to showcase drawings, notes, and other memorabilia from children or other important people in your life.

Finished size as shown: 50 x 36"

MATERIALS

15 pieces 8 x 10" white bristol board

15 notes or letters

15 white wooden 8 x 10" picture frames

Landscaping wire mesh

2 small screw eyes

No. 5 braided picture wire

30 to 50-lb. frame hanger and nail

TOOLS

Cutting mat

Straightedge

Pencil

Utility knife

Acid-free tape

White duct tape

Wire cutters

Staple gun and staples

Measuring tape

Hammer

1. On a work surface, place one piece of bristol board face down on your cutting mat. Center a note on the back side of the board. Using your straightedge, outline the edges of the note with a pencil. Set the note aside. Draw a smaller box approximately ¼" in from all sides of the original box.

2. Using your utility knife and straightedge, cut out the smaller box. Place the note face down on this opening. Place acid-free tape along the top and bottom edges of the note to secure.

3. Repeat steps 1 and 2 for the remaining 14 notes.

4. Place the bristol board mats with attached notes in the frames.

5. On a large, flat work surface, place your framed notes side by side in three rows (five in each row). Once you've found a composition you like, flip the frames face down. Note that when the frames are facing down, they should be lined up in reverse order.

6. Make sure all the edges of the frames are aligned. Using duct tape, secure all of the frames together along the edges.

7. Place the landscaping wire mesh over the backs of the frames. With wire cutters, trim the edges of the wire mesh along the edges of the outermost frames. Using a staple gun, staple the wire mesh to the back edges of the frames.

8. With the measuring tape, measure vertically along the left side of your frame composition. Mark the center with a pencil on the wood frame. Repeat for the right side of the frame composition.

9. At each mark, twist the small screw eye in place by hand, being careful not to elongate the screw holes. The bottom of the screw eye's circular opening should just touch the surface of the wooden frame.

10. String one end of braided picture wire through one screw eye. Leave enough slack in the wire so that when it is pulled taut up against the back of the frame composition the center point of the wire reaches about halfway between the screw eyes and the top of the frame composition. Leave about 3" of extra wire at each end. Wrap both ends of the extra wire tightly around the hanging wire. Trim excess wire with wire cutters.

11. Hammer a 30 to 50-lb. frame hanger into the wall and hang the composition.

Decoupaged London

paula smail
los angeles, california

"Who I am and how I live (and decorate) is a reflection of the twists and turns of my life, the people and things I love, the places I've visited, and the lessons I may or may not have learned along the way," says designer Paula Smail. "People's houses should be decorated with this in mind. I hate it when I walk into a person's home and I can't tell a darn thing about them."

Filled with decorative elements like an African feather headdress, a Warhol exhibition poster from Florence, and an array of photos from Vietnam, her current home is a veritable scrapbook of her life and travels. Born and raised in Cape Town, South Africa, Paula worked as an au pair in her teen years in Germany, Brazil, and Italy, moved to London after college, and then to New York. She now lives in West Hollywood, California, where she designs her own line of textiles for her company, Henry Road.

Paula's colorful journey is reflected throughout her hue-imbued home. However, there was one home appliance that almost threw off her decorative pursuits: the "big white fridge." But when she saw, in a magazine, a common kitchen refrigerator elegantly covered with a map, she knew she found a solution. Not only would bringing color and pattern to this unlikely candidate elevate its mere utilitarian status, but it would also give her another opportunity to share some of her memories—ultimately transforming what she once considered an eyesore into the room's focal point.

Deciding on a map to envelop the refrigerator was a no-brainer: the *A-Z London* book. London was a common stomping ground for South Africans, so Paula's move there after finishing at the University of Cape Town in the late 1980s was not surprising. In those pre-iPhone years, Paula remembers it being impossible to get around without this trusty atlas. She calls herself "the proud owner of a dog-eared version." Seeing the atlas pages every day on her refrigerator takes her back to a time when she was a new college graduate launching a career in public relations. It also serves as a poignant reminder of how far she's come.

Decoupaged London

Commemorating a place she once lived, Paula Smail decoupaged her refrigerator with a map of London. Of course, you can choose a map of any place that's meaningful to you. Note that atlases are best to illustrate a continuous map across a large surface area like a refrigerator because the maps are usually spread out over many pages.

Finished size as shown:
32 ⅞ x 67 ½ x 33 ⅝"

MATERIALS

2 copies of an atlas

16-ounce jar matte Mod Podge decoupage glue

1 quart matte or gloss polyurethane sealer

TOOLS

All-purpose cleaner

Degreaser (optional)

Paper towels

Measuring tape

8 ½ x 11" sheet of paper

Scissors

Cutting mat

Small utility knife

Straightedge

Three 1 ½"-wide paintbrushes

Clean cloth (optional)

1. With all-purpose cleaner, thoroughly clean the entire surface of your refrigerator. For particularly sticky areas, use a degreaser.

2. With a measuring tape, measure the surface area of your refrigerator. Sketch the dimensions on a sheet of paper.

3. Carefully cut out whole pages from your atlas. On a cutting mat, use a utility knife and straightedge to make sure all edges are straight and perpendicular. You'll need two copies of your atlas because adjoining map sections are printed on opposite sides of the same page.

4. On a clear and clean area of your floor, lay the map pages out in a sequential pattern to match the dimensions of the surface area of the refrigerator. To be safe, include more map pages to cover a slightly larger area.

5. Starting with the top left map page, apply an even layer of decoupage glue with a paintbrush to the back of each map page and place it on the fridge one page at a time. Gently use a clean paintbrush or cloth to smooth over each page to get out as many air bubbles as possible without tearing the paper. Wrap the maps over the top edge of the doors and around the corners. Cut out excess paper at the edges and around the door handles with a utility knife.

6. When you have covered the entire surface desired, let dry completely.

7. With a new paintbrush, apply two coats of sealer, allowing the sealer to dry thoroughly between coats.

Locker Hook Rug

christine schmidt
san francisco, california

In her stationery and home accessories business

called Yellow Owl Workshop, Christine Schmidt tries to keep things eco-friendly by using water-based inks and recycled paper and by creating the majority of her products by hand. Likewise, she applies her green sensibilities in her home whenever possible. For example, she hooked her kitchen rug out of scrap fabric leftover from other craft projects as well as repurposed fabric salvaged from an old blanket, duvet covers, and her husband Evan Gross's work shirts. "They were from his old lawyer job. He doesn't need them as much anymore, so I found a use for them," recalls Christine.

The design of the rug is based on Josef Albers's series "Homage to the Square." Gathering the fabric scraps and arranging them by color brought Christine back to her days as a freshman learning color theory at Corcoran College of Art and Design in Washington, D.C. Hooking the rug with a locker hook—a "down-home weaving method," Christine explains—brought her back to her childhood in Kansas City, Missouri, where her mother, a grade-school art teacher, taught her and her three sisters a variety of crafts, from scrap-paper cardmaking to weaving on cardboard looms.

For Christine, her kitchen rug is more than just a soft place for her feet; it's also an homage to her influential teachers and her inspiring mother, Mary Beth Schmidt.

Locker Hook Rug

Christine Schmidt gave her husband's old shirts and some scrap fabric a second life by weaving them into a rug using a locker-hook technique. If the clothes you have available for re-purposing don't feel cohesive in color, consider dyeing them in a palette you like.

Finished size as shown: 24 x 36"

MATERIALS

2 yards white cotton fabric

1 ¼ yards tan cotton fabric

1 yard yellow cotton fabric

¾ yard orange cotton fabric

3.75 mesh rug canvas (about 3 or 4 squares per inch), at least 28 x 40"

100-yard package cotton locker hooking twine, cut to 36" lengths

Iron-on rug binding

TOOLS

Scissors

Permanent marker

Locker hook

Clothespins

Iron and ironing board

1. With your scissors, cut your fabrics into long, 1"-wide strips. Fold the last ½" at each end of each fabric strip and make a ½" buttonhole incision in the center. You can stack several fabric strips on top of each other to accomplish this quickly. Set aside.

2. Trim your rug canvas to 28 x 40". With a permanent marker, draw lines 2" in from the perimeter of the rug canvas to make a rectangle that measures 24 x 36". You will draw your rug design within this rectangle. Looking at the rug vertically, draw three nesting squares on the top two-thirds of the canvas.

3. Keeping your canvas in a vertical orientation, thread cotton twine through the eye of your locker hook and knot it to the bottom right square of your rug canvas (within the rectangle), leaving a 4" tail.

4. Holding a strip of white fabric against the back of the canvas, use the hook end of your threaded locker hook to

⟫⟶

pull a loop of fabric through to the front of the canvas, leaving the loop on the shaft of the locker tool. Moving in a horizontal direction, continue to pull a loop through each canvas opening. When you have between 4 and 8 loops on your locker hook, pull the threaded locker hook through the row of loops on the front side of the canvas. This will secure the row of loops to the canvas. Load another 4 to 8 loops of fabric and pull the threaded locker hook through the loops again. Repeat, creating locked loops and moving back and forth up the rows, until you reach the drawn squares.

5. When you have come to the last 4" of your fabric strip, place the end of a new fabric strip on top of the 4" tail, aligning the buttonhole slits. Pull the opposite end of the new fabric strip though both buttonhole slits to create a knot. This knot will be hidden on the back side of the rug. Continue with locker hooking by repeating Step 4. If you need to add a new length of twine, tie the tail of the previous twine to the new length

with a single knot. Trim both ends of the knot to 1".

6. When you reach the drawn squares, begin making loops around the perimeter and working your way inward. Continuing with your white fabric, make a white perimeter around the largest square. To begin making the tan square, knot the tan and white fabrics together through their buttonhole slits at the point of change. Trim both ends of the knot to 1" and locker hook tan section. Repeat the same process when you reach the areas designated for the yellow and orange squares.

7. When you have completed your design, knot the fabric strip and cotton twine together two times and trim, leaving a 1" tail. Fold the extra 2" perimeter of rug canvas toward the back of the canvas and secure with clothespins. Tuck any tails near the edges underneath the folded canvas.

8. Cut two 24" pieces and two 36" pieces of iron-on rug binding. Place the 24" pieces along the short edges of the rug, and 36" pieces along the

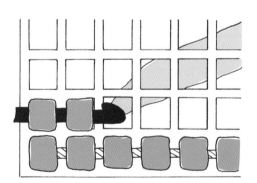

Step 4: Pull loops of fabric through to the front of the canvas, leaving the loops on the shaft of the locker hook.

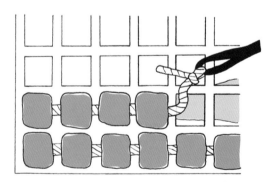

Step 4: When you have between 4 and 8 loops on your locker hook, pull the threaded hook through the loops to secure them to the canvas.

Christine demonstrates weaving around the perimeter of the design .

long edges of the rug. Iron the binding in place according to the package instructions.

9. With a permanent marker, dot the edge of every other hole at the short ends of the rug.

10. Thread twine through the eye of your locker hook. Holding the end of the twine in one hand, pull the threaded locker hook through the first marked hole at the far left of one edge, leaving a 4" tail. Insert the hook through the hole three more times, and then while holding the ends of the loops with one hand, wrap the twine several times around the top of the loops near the hole to create a tassel. Remove the twine from the locker hook. Loosen a couple wraps at the top of the tassel, insert the end of the twine through them, and pull tight to secure. Clip the loops at the end of the tassel. The ends will be trimmed after all the tassels are attached.

11. Repeat Step 10 until every marked hole has a tassel. Repeat for the opposite edge.

12. Trim all tassel ends to equal length.

Heritage Flag

christiana coop
san francisco, california

More than just a symbol of Great Britain, the British flag (known as the Union Jack) is also a prominent image in popular culture—gracing everything from car seat covers to underwear. Although Christiana Coop appreciates the flag's design, it also carries a strong sense of nostalgia for her. The Union Jack flag has been an icon in her family since before she was born, even adorning the top of her parents' wedding cake.

Prior to moving to the United States in 1970, Christiana's mother, Angela Coop, called Yorkshire in northern England her home. After she married and had two children, Jonathan and Christiana, the family visited England regularly. Christiana still holds many fond memories of those trips, including playing in the garden at her grandfather's home in West Yorkshire, meeting her great aunts and uncles and hearing stories about her mother's childhood, exploring castles along the Welsh coast, and a particularly special visit to London when she was eight that heightened her obsession with the royal family.

Though the trips became less frequent after her grandfather died in 2001, Christiana visited England in 2009, and was immediately flooded by warm recollections of her childhood visits there. When she returned home to San Francisco, she was inspired to make a large-scale interpretive version of the Union Jack flag out of remnant rolls of wallpaper. Hung on the wall above her bed, the flag—and England—are never far away.

Heritage Flag

A nod to her British heritage and her fond childhood memories of England, Christiana Coop made a large-scale Union Jack flag from pieces of patterned wallpaper adhered to Gator board. The wallpaper puts a contemporary spin on the flag while maintaining the integrity of its design. This project can be adapted to just about any flag or other bold graphic.

Finished size as shown: 3 x 6'

MATERIALS

4 x 8' piece ¾"-thick Gator board

Blue or black patterned roll of wallpaper (21" wide x 16' long)

White or cream patterned roll of wallpaper (21" wide x 12' long)

Red patterned roll of wallpaper (21" wide x 12' long)

Wallpaper paste

¾"-wide hook-and-loop (Velcro) tape

TOOLS

Tarp

Large cutting mat

Measuring tape

Utility knife

Straightedge

Scissors

2"-wide paintbrush

Squeegee

Sponge

Pencil

1. On a large, flat work surface, lay down your tarp. Place the cutting mat on top. With your measuring tape, utility knife, and straightedge, measure and trim the 4 x 8' Gator board to 3 x 6'.

2. With scissors, cut one strip of blue or black wallpaper 3½' long. This will be the background of the Union Jack flag. Place this strip on top of the Gator board, to the far left. The wallpaper will need to wrap around the sides of the Gator board. Cut three additional strips of wallpaper. For each additional strip, align the wallpaper along the edge of the prior strip, lining up the pattern. Each strip needs to be at least 3½' long, but some may need to be longer to line up the pattern. When you have finished cutting all the strips, center them on the Gator board.

3. Load your brush with wallpaper paste. Starting with the far left strip, brush the back side and gently lay it on the board. Slowly pull your squeegee along the front side of the wallpaper, starting at the top and working your way down, to smooth out any air bubbles. Wipe any excess paste with a damp sponge. Wrap the edges around the sides of the Gator board. Repeat for the remaining three strips. Allow wallpaper to dry.

≫⟶

Overall dimensions and design of the Union Jack flag.

4. With your utility knife and straightedge, trim the white or cream wallpaper into two pieces: one 12 x 72" (horizontal section) and the other 12 x 36" (vertical section). These pieces will make the white cross on the flag. Referring to the diagram on the following page, cut the four diagonal pieces (according to the dimensions) from the white or cream wallpaper. Position all of the pieces on the board, marking their placement with a pencil.

5. Starting with the horizontal strip, brush the back side with wallpaper paste and gently lay the strip on the board according to the marks you made. Slowly pull your squeegee along the front side of the wallpaper to smooth out any air bubbles and to get rid of excess paste. Repeat for the remaining pieces. Allow wallpaper to dry.

6. Using your straightedge and utility knife, trim the red wallpaper into two pieces: one 7 ¼ x 72" (horizontal section) and the other 7 ¼ x 36" (vertical section). Referring to the diagram on

the following page, cut the four diagonal pieces (according to the dimensions) from the red wallpaper. Position all of the pieces on the board according to the diagram, marking their placement with a pencil.

7. Starting with the horizontal strip, brush the back side with wallpaper paste and gently lay the strip on the board according to the marks you made. Use your squeegee again to smooth out any air bubbles and to get rid of excess paste. Repeat for the remaining pieces.

8. Carefully wipe down the wallpaper with a damp sponge to help get rid of any paste that may have gotten onto the face of the wallpaper. Allow to dry overnight.

9. To hang, adhere one piece of the adhesive-backed hook-and-loop tape to each corner of the board and stick to the wall.

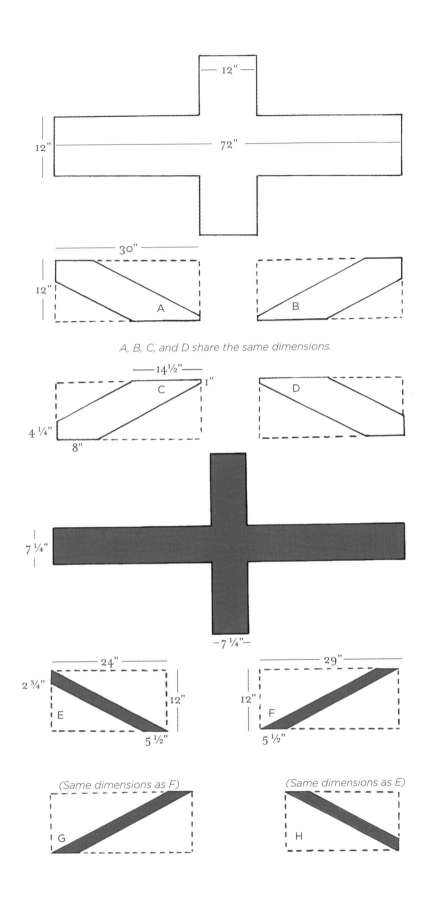

12"

72"

12"

30"

12"

A

B

A, B, C, and D share the same dimensions.

14½"

1"

C

D

4¼"

8"

7¼"

—7¼"—

24"

2¾"

12"

E

5½"

29"

12"

F

5½"

(Same dimensions as F)

G

(Same dimensions as E)

H

City Rubbings

susan connor
new york, new york

Walking around New York City, surface designer
Susan Connor has always been mesmerized by the forms she encounters—from
graceful cornerstones and signage with dated typefaces to mundane manhole
covers and subway grates. She relishes the details that people often miss as they
walk along the street. Born in Cambridge, Massachusetts, and growing up in
Lexington outside of Boston, Susan was surrounded as a child by remind-
ers of early American history. When she moved to New York to live with her
boyfriend, Kurt Wildermuth, in 2006, her attraction to things with history
helped ground her. "Seeing municipal signs, wrought-iron elements, and
beautiful old buildings in my neighborhood helped me get acclimated to my
new environment," she says. "They made me feel more comfortable, more at
home."

Susan's neighborhood, midtown Manhattan, is filled largely with banks
and law firms, rife with institutional signs and placards. With paper and a
variety of mediums, including conté crayons and graphite sticks, she makes
rubbings of these elements, moving the paper around to yield abstract com-
positions, and displays them in her home. For one rubbing, she gravitated toward an *S* that she describes as "blobby, bouncy, and amorphous"—akin to her
personality—on a law firm sign on 46th Street and Park Avenue. Not to leave
Kurt out, she found a *K* that felt "angular, cubist, and masculine" on a bank
placard on 3rd Avenue and 51st Street. Expressing her love for 1950s typogra-
phy, she rubbed a sans serif *51* from a retaining wall in front of Tudor City.

Indeed, every rubbing has a story, including its discovery and history
and the people she interacted with as she created it. She laughs as she recalls
how people watch her do the rubbings and wonder if she is defacing public or
private property. Being out on the street, engaging both buildings and people,
helped her settle into her neighborhood. Above all, Susan loves how the rubbings record history and how their often ghostly look makes a subtle statement
about the impermanency of things.

City Rubbings

Susan Connor documents her New York neighborhood through rubbings displayed in her home. Though Susan has a preference for typefaces on signage and building numbers, you can essentially create a rubbing from any raised surface. This is a great way to celebrate special places, for example, your hometown, college campus, or honeymoon destination.

Finished sizes as shown:
11 x 17" and 8 ½ x 11"

MATERIALS

8 ½ x 11" or larger archival paper

Graphite sticks, wax crayons, conté crayons, and/or colored pastels

Frames (optional)

TOOLS

Spray bottle with water

Paper towels

Painter's tape

Spray fixative

Flat portfolio case

1. Find a surface with elevated elements (such as a sign with embossed letters). Clean the surface by spraying with water and wiping with a dry paper towel to ensure that the paper doesn't get dirty.

2. Lay a sheet of paper over the sign. Using tape, secure the paper to the sign, making sure that at least two sides of the paper are secure and won't blow around. Leave a good amount of paper around the sides so that it can be trimmed down later.

3. Using the side of your graphite stick or crayon, gently stroke the surface of the paper. The more strokes you make, the clearer the image will become. Use the tip of the crayon for more detail. Remember not to press too hard because you might tear through the paper.

4. Once you are satisfied with the image, gently remove the tape, making sure you do not leave any on the surface you were using.

5. Apply spray fixative to seal the image. Once it has dried, place in the portfolio case for safe travel.

6. Frame or hang as is.

Family Banner

samantha hahn
brooklyn, new york

The office in Samantha Hahn and Dave Moldawer's
Brooklyn apartment was undergoing a transformation—swapping a swivel
chair for a rocking chair, a computer desk for a changing table. A baby was
on the way. For some first-time parents, picking a decorating scheme for
baby's nursery can be a daunting task, but for Samantha and Dave it was a job
they welcomed with ease. As a freelance illustrator and art teacher for young
children, Samantha has demonstrated many times over how primary colors are
the building blocks for understanding color theory. So it's no surprise, then,
that primary colors would also be the color foundation for their new baby's
(Henry's) room.

Dave is a book editor and, along with Samantha, believed that the space
ought to share a meaningful narrative. They also wanted to surround Henry
with the people who love him—but they didn't want to represent family in a
traditional way, merely through photographs. So Samantha came up with the
idea to create a family banner with each member's silhouette on a decorative
flag.

In the design of the family banner, Samantha has each family represented
on either side of Henry's name. All the silhouettes are turned inward to face
Henry's name. On Samantha's side is her silhouette; her brother, Aaron;
mother, Marika; and dad, Lewis. Dave's silhouette is on the opposite side,
followed by his mother, Susan; older sister, Laurie; and father, Richard. Little
touches on some silhouettes make it clear who's who. For example, the ban-
dana around a male silhouette is Aaron, Samantha's brother, an art student
known for wearing the accessory around his neck. And everyone in both families knows that the silhouette with a flower is Samantha's because she is fond
of picking wildflowers and planting them behind her ear. The male silhouette
closest to Henry's name would, by natural deduction, be his father, Dave. But
even still, his silhouette sports his trademark dark-rimmed glasses.

Family Banner

Stressing the importance of family, Samantha Hahn decorated her baby's nursery with flags bearing the silhouettes of her and her husband's families. When tracing a person's profile, Samantha notes that it's important to outline as many distinctive features (such as curly hair or long eyelashes) as you can. Embellishing the silhouettes with distinguishing details like glasses is another effective way to personalize them.

Finished size as shown: 7 x 23"

MATERIALS

Colored acrylic felt

White acrylic felt

Ribbon or yarn for threading through flags

TOOLS

Digital camera

Computer and printer

Copier (optional)

Fine-tip scissors

Pen with white ink

Cardboard for triangle template

Fine-point permanent marker

Alphabet stencils

Glue gun and glue sticks

Note: Samantha used six colors—light blue, dark blue, yellow, red, white, and black. Depending on how many letters are in the child's name and how many silhouettes you wish to make, you might use more or fewer colors. Also, silhouettes are traditionally black on a white ground, but you can play with any combination you prefer, as long as there is a strong contrast.

1. Using a digital camera, take photos of each family member against a white wall. Take each photograph in portrait (lengthwise), including only the person's head to his or her shoulder in the shot. Print 4 x 6" photographs. Each person should have a profile image that measures roughly 3 x 4".

2. If you want to make the size of each profile uniform, you can enlarge or reduce the prints on a copier, or you can resize the images on your computer before printing.

3. With fine-tip scissors, cut out each photograph or photocopied image. Be sure to catch all the details of each person's profile.

4. Decide what color felt you want for each person's profile. Place your first piece of felt on your work surface. Decide which direction you want the profile to face and then flip over for tracing. With your permanent marker (or white ink pen for dark-colored felt), carefully trace the reversed profile onto the felt. Cut out the silhouette with scissors, again catching the details of that person's profile. Repeat for all remaining profiles.

5. From the cardboard, cut out a triangle with a 6" base and a 7" height. This will be your flag template.

6. Decide what felt colors you want to use for your flags. With your permanent marker (or white ink pen for dark-colored felt), trace around your cardboard flag template onto the pieces of felt. Cut enough flags for each profile plus the letters of the child's name.

7. Using the alphabet stencils, trace each letter of the child's name in reverse onto a piece of white felt. Cut out the letters.

8. With your glue gun, place glue along the edge on the back of each silhouette. With the flag pointing down, place one silhouette on each flag.

9. Using scraps of felt, cut embellishments to decorate each person's profile. Glue them onto the profiles or flags.

10. Glue the felt letters one at a time, one letter on each flag. Again, make sure the flags are pointing down.

11. Once the glue has dried on all flags, cut a ½" vertical slit at the top corners of each flag. Thread ribbon or yarn through each flag and hang.

Folklore Chair

diana fayt

san francisco, california

Diana Fayt's parents, Laszlo Fajt and Zsuzanna

Roder, were two unlikely characters who met at a café on the iconic corner of Hollywood and Vine in Hollywood, California. Having escaped the Hungarian Revolution of 1956, they led a new life in the United States that was a far cry from the one they once knew in Hungary. Though they assimilated by adopting the American names Les and Susanna Fayt, they were still resourceful people who held onto practices and traditions from the Old World. It isn't surprising that Diana's childhood in Sunnyvale, California, was in many ways no different from one she would have experienced had her parents met and lived in Hungary. Diana recalls watching her mother make clothes from whole cloth. Her father purchased slaughtered pigs and she assisted in hand-cranking pork sausages in their garage.

In 1983, Diana, then nineteen, wanted to explore her origins and experience life in her parents' homeland. She stayed for seven months and learned to speak Hungarian under the tutelage of her six-year-old cousin. She traversed communist Hungary with a pack of former circus stars, including her mother's sister, who had stayed behind during the revolution. When Diana returned to California, her mother was astounded at her proficiency in Hungarian. Throughout Diana's childhood and teenage years, her mother had misinterpreted her shyness as disdain for Hungarian culture and language.

Two decades later, Diana is now an accomplished ceramic artist, etching illustrations into clay and weaving stories about her life into her work in subtle ways. In 2007, she decided to openly examine her life and roots when she created pieces for an art show she called "Folklore." In the folklore chair she created for the show, Diana used common Hungarian folk staples such as roosters and roses. Roosters are found in everyday Hungarian dinnerware, while roses make Diana nostalgic as many of the older women in her family grew rose gardens. For Diana, roses symbolize the conversation among Hungarian women. Recreating these ubiquitous folk images has become a welcome exercise and a challenge for Diana, allowing her to document and reinterpret her culture through a contemporary lens.

Folklore Chair

Diana Fayt dedicates a chair to her Hungarian heritage by screen-printing hand-drawn folklore motifs onto the fabric covering the seat cushion. If desired, substitute another motif that is meaningful to you. Note that with screen-printing, you can repeat a pattern or design. So you can make your design on a smaller screen than the one listed below, but you will need to print multiple passes to fill your fabric. You will also need to buy a smaller squeegee to fit within your screen.

Finished size as shown: Chair is 18" wide x 15" deep x 35" high; seat cover is 18 x 15"

MATERIALS

Vintage wood chair with removable cushion

Black chalkboard paint

1 yard medium-weight cotton fabric in a natural color

8 ounces screen drawing fluid

8 ounces screen filler

2 hinge pins

36 x 24" piece medium-density fibreboard (MDF available at hardware stores)

Two 19 x 24" sheets clear acetate

Black water-based screen-printing ink for fabric

White pencil

TOOLS

Drop cloth

Screwdriver

Cloth or rag

Wood cleaner

Sandpaper

Tack cloth

2"-wide paintbrush

Iron and ironing board

Fabric scissors

Fabric marker

Photocopier

30 x 20" assembled silk-screen frame with 230 mesh

2"-wide masking tape

Soft-lead pencil

Old newspapers

Fine-tip, pointed paintbrush

Hair dryer (optional)

Screen-printing squeegee with 22" blade

Sink with faucet that has a spray attachment

Soft toothbrush

Ruler

Staple gun and staples

Prepare Chair

1. Lay down your drop cloth and place the chair on top. Using a screwdriver, remove the seat from the chair, putting the screws aside and discarding the fabric covering. Set aside.

2. With a damp cloth and wood cleaner, thoroughly clean the chair and remove any dust or dirt that may be on the surface. Lightly sand the surface of the chair and wipe the dust off with a tack cloth.

⟫ ➔

3. Apply the chalkboard paint with a paintbrush in a light, even coat over the entire chair. Apply a second coat and let dry overnight.

4. With an iron and ironing board, press the fabric and lay it face up on your work surface. Place the cushion, face up, on the fabric. With your fabric scissors, trim the fabric so it extends 4" beyond the edges of the cushion on all sides. With a fabric marker, mark the corners of your cushion. Set the fabric and cushion aside.

Screen-Print Fabric

5. Make a photocopy of Diana's folklore drawing on page 153, enlarging the original image by 290% (the resized image will be roughly 19 ¼ x 9" and will be printed twice on your fabric). You can also use your own folklore image or motif (preferably a graphic image with a definite outline) and make a photocopy, resizing the original image to an appropriate size for the chair seat.

6. On a large work surface, set your silk-screen frame mesh side down. Place your photocopied artwork, print side down, on the center of the screen. Tape all four corners of the artwork to the screen. Turn the screen over. With a soft-lead pencil, trace the design. Remove the paper and tape.

7. On your work surface, lean the screen at a slight angle against a wall, mesh side up, with newspapers beneath it. Use a fine-tip, pointed paintbrush and drawing fluid to paint over the traced design. Apply three or four coats of drawing fluid to ensure the holes are filled in. Any solid areas on the design must be painted solid. (If you are not satisfied with how your design looks on the screen, you can wash it out, allow the screen to dry completely, and begin again.) When your design is finished, allow the screen to dry completely in a level, flat position. Make sure nothing is touching the drawing fluid. You can use a hair dryer to speed the drying time.

8. Shake the container of screen filler thoroughly. With your screen flat on your work surface, mesh side up, scoop a generous amount of screen filler in a line across the top of your screen. With your squeegee placed at the top, pull it at a 45-degree angle down across the screen in one pass to spread a thin, even layer of screen filler over the entire screen. Place the screen in a horizontal position and allow the screen filler to dry overnight.

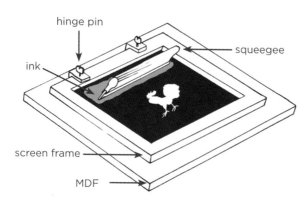

Step 13: To screen print your design, apply pressure and drag the squeegee at about a 45-degree angle across the design toward you.

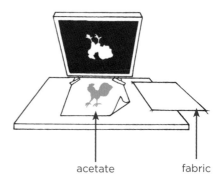

Step 14: Lift the screen to reveal the design printed on the acetate. Take your fabric and position it under the clear acetate. Remove the acetate to print onto the fabric.

9. Bring your screen to a sink with a faucet that has a spray attachment. Spray cold water at a high pressure directly at the design. Do this on both sides of the screen. The drawing fluid will wash away completely. This unfilled mesh will be your stencil that will allow ink to pass through. Use a soft toothbrush to remove any filler or fluid in the design that does not come out during the wash. If you see pinholes in the filler area, dab more filler using a fine-tip paintbrush. Let dry completely.

10. Place your screen on your work surface, mesh side down. Place masking tape along the four edges of your screen (where the frame meets the mesh). Half of the tape should go on the screen, and the other half should go on the mesh. Set aside.

11. Screw the two hinge pins along the top of your MDF about 10" apart on center.

12. Place your screen (oriented horizontally) on center with the hinge pins, screwing them into place. Raise the screen. Place a sheet of clear acetate in the center of the MDF. Tape the top two corners of the acetate.

13. Lower your screen. Scoop about ½ cup of screen-printing ink in a line above the design. Holding the squeegee at about a 45-degree angle above the ink line, apply pressure and drag the squeegee across the design toward you. This will pull ink across the design and through the open mesh. Turn the squeegee around and, using the same side of the blade, pull the squeegee up and away from you with no pressure. This is a process called "flooding," which leaves a thin layer of ink on the screen to prevent it from drying.

14. Place the squeegee aside on newspaper and lift the screen. You should have printed your design onto the clear acetate. Take your fabric and place it under the clear acetate. Keeping the cushion's

corner markings in mind, position your fabric so the design will print centered on the top half of the cushion fabric. (Note that the design needs to be printed twice onto the fabric, once at the top and once at the bottom.) Tape your fabric down on all four corners. Remove the clear acetate. Repeat Step 13 to print on the fabric.

15. Remove your screen-printed fabric. Tape a new sheet of clear acetate onto the MDF and repeat Step 13. Repeat Step 14, however, when placing the preprinted fabric under the clear acetate, make sure the ink on the fabric has dried completely, blow-drying it if necessary. Also, you will be aligning the design on the acetate, with the preprinted design on the fabric this time, to print the bottom half of the cushion fabric.

16. Wash your screen immediately with water and let dry. Remove the screen-printed fabric and let dry. Once it is dry, iron on high heat to heat set the ink.

Attach Fabric and Finish Chair

17. Place the chair cushion on your work surface. Lay the printed fabric face up on top of the cushion, making sure the design is centered. Flip the cushion and fabric over. Pull the fabric over the side, one side at a time, and using a staple gun, staple 1½" from the edge, at the center of each side. Turn the chair cushion over and check to see that the design is centered. Make any adjustments as necessary. Continue stapling around the cushion, working from the center to the corners on each side. Pull the fabric tightly while simultaneously making sure the design is properly positioned on the seat. Trim the excess fabric 1" past the staples.

18. Secure the cushion to the chair with the original screws.

19. Write a message or draw an image with the white pencil on the front of the chair.

Needlepoint Racquets

amy holbrook
brooklyn, new york

As Amy Holbrook learned, creative epiphanies

can happen when you put together your present and past interests—including the unlikely pairing of tennis and needlepoint. Tennis was always a family affair for Amy growing up—she, her parents, brother, and sister all played. In fact, Amy began learning the sport at the early age of five.

During college, Amy's interest in tennis faded as she discovered a new passion for the Italian language. After graduation, she moved to Italy. Inspired by the large needlepoint tapestries she saw at her friends' homes there, she started taking up the craft as a way to relieve stress and to pass time during flights back and forth between the United States and Italy. As she scoured craft shops for needlepoint projects, she quickly realized that the majority of the kits on the market had kitschy themes that didn't appeal to her style and modern sensibilities. That realization led her to found AMH Design, a contemporary needlepoint company.

During a recent visit to her mother's home in Connecticut, Amy came across some old tennis racquets and noticed that the head of a racquet resembles a needlepoint frame. At first, she wanted to needlepoint directly onto the racquet, but the spaces of the grid were too large. So she simply cut out a needlepoint plastic canvas and attached it to the racquet's head. Now two racquets, one needlepointed with her initials and the other with the year she moved into her apartment, are on display at the entry of her home in Brooklyn, New York. Amy admits that a third interest is also woven into the design: the colors white, brown, red, and green are a nod to the signature palette of 1970s Gucci, her favorite Italian fashion company.

Needlepoint Racquets

Amy Holbrook combines her love of needlepoint and tennis in this project. You can follow Amy's design and place your initials on one racquet and a special year on another. Or you can plan your own unique design.

Finished size as shown: 23 ½ x 26"

MATERIALS

Two 7-count plastic canvas sheets, 7 holes per inch

2 vintage wooden tennis racquets

2 sheets 8 ½ x 11" graph paper

Paternayan tapestry wool: 80 yards in white (#260) and 50 yards each of red (#970), green (#632), and brown (#430)

Wood glue

2 small flat-head nails

TOOLS

Double-sided tape

Crayon

Scissors

Paper towels

Charted letters and numbers (see page 154)

Size 18 tapestry needle

Needle threader

Pencil

Fine-tooth handsaw

Wood chisel

Hammer

Note: This project uses the half-cross stitch, a basic needlepoint technique that consists of single slanted stitches (see illustrations on the following page). When making a horizontal row of half-cross stitches, you normally begin from right to left by bringing the needle up through one hole, crossing diagonally to the row below, and back up through the hole directly above. In your first row, each stitch should slant in a southwesterly direction on the front of your canvas and appear as vertical lines on the backside. As you continue stitching onto the row above, you will move from left to right, bringing the needle up through one hole, crossing diagonally to the row above and back up through the hole directly below. If you are right-handed, start stitching on the lower right corner of the design and work to the left. If you are left-handed, start on the lower left corner and work to the right. Work stitches from the bottom of your design area and move up.

1. On a flat work surface, lay a plastic canvas sheet on top of one tennis racquet's head and secure with double-sided tape. Using a crayon, slowly trace the inner outline of the racquet's head onto the plastic canvas. Cut around the lines you traced so that the canvas fits snugly within the racquet's head. Adjust accordingly. Wipe off any excess crayon with a paper towel. Repeat for the second racquet. (Trace and cut each canvas separately because the racquet heads may be different sizes.)

2. Use graph paper to design your racquet. You can choose from the letters and numbers provided (see page 154) to

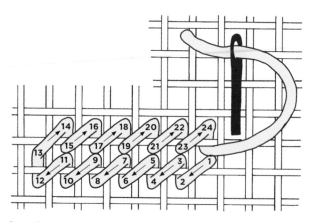

Step 3: Making horizontal rows of stitches.

help chart your initials and the date, leaving at least one or two squares between each letter or number. In this project, the red and green stripes are 7 x 24 stitches and the brown stripe is 9 x 24 stitches. The stripes are the same dimensions at the top and bottom of the racquet.

3. Start the project by stitching the brown stripe in the center of the canvas. Cut an 18" strand of tapestry wool, and thread one end through the tapestry needle, leaving about a 1" tail. Hold the tail in place on the back of the canvas while you stitch and cover the tail with your stitches to ensure that your wool doesn't come loose. Begin stitching the brown stripe from the bottom of your canvas, making a horizontal row of stitches from right to left. (If you are left-handed, work stitches from left to right.) Be careful not to pull the wool too tightly because it will make the stitches thinner, causing the canvas to show.

Using the illustration above as a guide, bring your needle up through hole 1 and stitch diagonally to the left, to the row below, inserting the needle down through hole 2. Bring your needle back up through the hole directly above, hole 3, and repeat. To start the next row, bring the needle up through the canvas at hole 13, directly above hole 12. Next, stitch diagonally to the right, to the row above, inserting the needle down through hole 14. Then bring your needle back up through the canvas at hole 15, and repeat.

When you have 3 to 4" of wool left on your needle,

secure the wool by bringing the needle to the back side of the canvas and running it under four or five stitches. Cut off the remaining tail. Rethread the needle and continue stitching until the stripe is completed.

4. Stitch the red and green stripes on the canvas according to the instructions in Step 3.

5. When stitching your letters and numbers, you will want to stitch in vertical rows from the bottom of your design area and move up. (If you are stitching correctly, the back of your work will have small horizontal stitches.) When you finish a letter or number, secure the yarn by running the needle under four or five stitches on the back side of the canvas. Use the illustrations below as a guide.

6. Fill in the background on the racquet with white wool by making horizontal rows of stitches starting at the bottom of the racquet. When you have completed the design, use white wool to stitch around the outside edges so that the canvas is no longer visible.

7. Use some of the remaining wool to tie the canvas to the racquet strings. Choose four places on the racquet head (two around the top arc and two around the bottom) and run the wool through the back of a few stitches, then tie it to the racquet strings, trimming off the excess wool.

8. Once you have finished both racquets, lay them one on top of the other in a crossed position as shown on page 108. Use a pencil to mark the intersection on each racquet, outlining notches that are half the depth of the wood handle.

9. Following the marks you made, use a handsaw to carefully make the cuts. Next, use a chisel and hammer to remove the wood in between the two cuts to make the indentation. Repeat with the second racquet. Test-fit the racquets and make sure that both racquets lie flush on your surface. Make any adjustments as necessary. Finally, cover the indentation on each racquet with wood glue and attach the racquets together. Let dry.

10. With a pencil, mark where you want to hang your racquets on the wall. Hammer two small flat-head nails into the wall just below the pencil markings and hang the racquets by their strings.

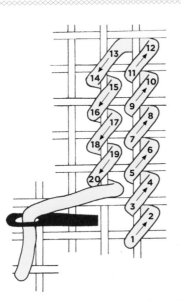

Step 5: Making vertical rows of stitches.

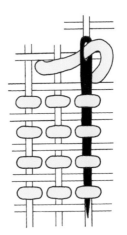

Step 5: Back of the needlepoint canvas showing small horizontal stitches. To secure the wool at the end of stitching, run the needle under four or five stitches.

Cityscape Collage

lorena siminovich
san francisco, california

When Lorena Siminovich was just four years

old, she called airplanes her second home. Exhibiting an independence far beyond her years, Lorena would travel alone between her mother's home in Argentina and her father's in Ecuador. It isn't surprising that by age sixteen Lorena wanted to travel abroad to Europe. But Lorena's mother told her that she had to wait until she turned eighteen to cross the Atlantic Ocean. Holding her mother to her word, on the day of her eighteenth birthday, Lorena hopped on a plane and spent one month touring London, Paris, Venice, Florence, Andalusia, and Barcelona.

Years later, in 2001, Lorena set up a new challenge—not simply to travel, but to uproot herself from her hometown and birthplace, Buenos Aires, and move to a city of seemingly endless possibilities: New York City. There, Lorena landed a job as a graphic designer for Galison, a stationery and gift company, and eventually rose through the ranks to become a vice president. Soon after arriving, Lorena discovered that Esteban Kerner, a childhood friend from Argentina, lived only a couple of blocks away from her in Brooklyn. The two began dating immediately and, in 2005, they married.

When Esteban's work relocated him to San Francisco in 2005, Lorena, a lover of metropolitan cities, welcomed the change. In fact, it led her to pursue her dream of working as a freelance illustrator and starting a children's décor company called Petit Collage. Known for her children's collages made with vintage paper on wood, Lorena made one for her young daughter, Matilda, when they moved into a new home in 2009. A collage she calls a "travelogue," this project showcases some of the trademark buildings, bridges, and monuments in cities that Lorena has visited or inhabited. She hopes it will inspire Matilda to explore the world. Indeed, Matilda is already well on her way—checking off cities like New York, Las Vegas, and Buenos Aires all before her first birthday.

Cityscape Collage

To share her love of international travel with her young daughter, Lorena Siminovich created a collage of building and monument forms from places she had visited and mounted it on wood. When you put together your collage, think of places you've been or places you hope to travel to someday or perhaps the houses of all of your friends growing up or your family members today—any theme will work.

Finished size as shown: 11 x 20"

MATERIALS

2 sheets 11 x 17" paper

15 to 30 pieces decorative paper varying in color, pattern, and size

11 x 20" piece ¾"-thick wood

8-ounce jar Mod Podge decoupage glue

2 sawtooth hangers

2 nails

TOOLS

Tape

Ruler

Scissors

Photocopier

Pencil

1 ½"-wide paintbrush

Permanent marker

Hammer

1. Tape the 11 x 17" sheets of paper together along one short edge. Measure and trim the joined papers to 11 x 20". This will be your paper template.

2. On page 155, choose building, bridge, and monument forms to use in your collage. Photocopy and resize the images and cut out the shapes with scissors. You can also draw your own building forms. Move the forms and shapes around on your paper template until you reach a final composition.

3. Taking them from the template one at a time, place your cut-out shapes on your decorative paper. Trace the edges of the shapes with a pencil and cut them out. Return the original shapes to the paper template, and place the shapes cut from the decorative paper in the corresponding area on the wood board.

4. Starting with the shapes in the bottom layer, use a paintbrush to apply the decoupage glue in long, thin strokes to the area on the wood board where the shape will be placed. Place each piece onto the wood board and apply another thin layer of glue. After all of the shapes have been attached to the wood, apply a light but complete layer of decoupage glue over the entire surface. Let dry.

5. Use a permanent marker to add any details to your building forms. Apply one or two additional coats of the decoupage glue.

6. Attach two sawtooth hangers to the back of the collage, about 1" below the top edge. Hammer two nails into the wall and hang.

Button Garland

brooke davies
los angeles, california

Growing up in rural Indiana, Brooke Davies

honed her button-collecting skills at an early age. More than three decades ago, before the days of eBay and Antiques Roadshow, her parents, Doug and Sandy Davies, started an antique auction business specializing in early Americana (nineteenth-century folk art and furniture). Traveling all over the Midwest, they met with people who wanted them to sell their salt and pepper shakers, cuckoo clocks, buttons, and other unusual collections. They would also sell out entire inventories of general stores that, among other things, included buttons on cards, laced together in large grosses, or in jars. Indeed, because of the antiques business, the Davies' home was well stocked with buttons made out of every material from Bakelite to wood. Although Brooke resented being dragged from auction to auction as a child, she realizes now it instilled in her an appreciation for collecting vintage goods.

The source of Brooke's button frenzy wasn't simply a by-product of her parents' antiques business either. Her grandmother, Charlene Young Turner, had a hand in it as well. Charlene lived with Brooke and her family and was a professional seamstress who ran a sewing business out of their home called Charlene's Skirts. One of Brooke's warmest memories of her grandmother is sharing a seat behind the sewing machine with her. She also recalls the many floral outfits Charlene created for her and her sister, Erin, during Charlene's "Laura Ashley" phase. And just as young girls often eye a pair of earrings or a brooch belonging to their mother or grandmother, Brooke and her sister coveted their grandmother's buttons. When Charlene died in 2004, Brooke inherited some of the very buttons that held such nostalgic meaning for her as a child.

Although Brooke earned a fine arts degree with a specialization in fashion from the Art Institute of Chicago, it's clear her education started long before she entered college. Since then she has run her own children's clothing line, called Clothpony, and now resides in Los Angeles with her husband, Darren Schmidt, and son, Calder. She continues to collect buttons during her travels, scouring flea markets and estate sales as her parents did. Every holiday season she carefully strings her buttons together to create garlands. With Calder's first Christmas approaching, she's looking forward to sharing the button tradition and recalling stories of her travels, the auctions, and her grandmother.

Button Garland

Brooke Davies created a garland for the holidays by stringing together buttons inherited from her family. You can mix store-bought buttons with sentimental buttons from old clothes or your stash to create your garland. In this project, the garlands are hung from a window frame, but you can modify the instructions to lengthen the garland for decorating a wall or tree.

Finished size as shown: 24" to 36"

MATERIALS (for one garland)

10 to 20 medium to large (1" to 2") vintage or contemporary buttons with 2 or 4 holes or a shank on the back

22-gauge silver craft wire on the roll

Vintage or contemporary glass holiday ornament

Small cup hook

TOOLS

Tape measure

Wire cutters

1. On a flat work surface, line up the buttons and play with the composition. Evenly space them about 1" apart. Mix and match different colors and sizes until you find a pattern you like.

2. Measure the length of craft wire you need, then add an extra 3". Cut the length with wire cutters.

3. Starting with the last button at the end of the garland, feed the end of your wire through one of the holes in the button or through the shank on the back. Pull the wire through, stopping about 2" before the end of the wire. If the button has holes, feed the length of the wire through a second hole in the button. If you are using a button with four holes, choose the hole diagonal from the first. For shank buttons, twist the wire together around the shank to secure.

4. Repeat Step 3 for all the buttons, spacing them approximately 1" apart. If the wire gets kinks while stringing, simply pull the wire from the top to straighten.

5. Once you have strung the buttons, feed the end of the wire through the ring at the top of the ornament. Bring the ornament as close to the last button as possible. Coil the wire tightly around itself so that it's hidden behind the button. With wire cutters, trim the wire end.

6. On the opposite end of the wire, create a ¾" loop. Coil the wire tightly around itself behind the top button. Trim the wire end.

7. Screw a cup hook to the top of the windowframe and hang the garland on the hook by its wire loop.

Two-Family Crest

chika eustace & jean lee
seattle, washington

Chika Eustace and Jean Lee have a lot in common.

They both have industrial design degrees. Chika met her boyfriend, Jared Randall, in the design program at Rhode Island School of Design. Jean met her boyfriend, Dylan Davis, in the design program at the University of Washington. Together, Chika and Jean maintain a partnership in their design company, Chikabird. And now, they share a common wall in their duplex.

It's hard to believe that just a few years ago these two were strangers on opposite coasts. Their paths eventually crossed after Chika and Jared moved across the country to Seattle. In 2002, Dylan, who was still an undergrad, began interning for Jared at a product design consultation firm. Dylan and Jared formed a friendship that soon transferred to their partners, Chika and Jean. When Chika's wallet design business, Chikabird, took off in 2005, a newly graduated Jean found herself with a job at the company. A year later, Jean became a partner. Together they've expanded their company to include notebooks and clothing.

Tired of renting, Jean and Dylan decided to look for a house in 2009. When they learned that duplexes were a more affordable option than a traditional single-family home for first-time home buyers, they could think of only one other couple to whom they'd want to live next door: Chika and Jared. Luckily, the idea was appealing to them as well. The two couples purchased and moved into their duplex, playfully dubbed "The Dupe," in the Ballard area of Seattle later that year. For both couples, being neighbors certainly has its perks, including a joint vegetable garden and many shared meals. Jean and Chika also turned one of their garages into the Chikabird business headquarters while the other became their workshop and bike parking area.

Inspired by European and Japanese family crests, Chika and Jean decided to create a modern version to represent the merging of their families, their common interests, and the spirit of their neighborhood. In the final design, an elevation of their home sits atop a shield in the shape of a ship's hull (a tribute to their Nordic community). Sprinkled throughout are icons burned or carved into the wood that are meaningful to the two couples: a rooster and quail symbolize Chikabird; man and woman icons stand for Ladies & Gentlemen, Dylan and Jean's company; scissors crossed by a Japanese saw represent their craftiness; a Cathrine Holm vintage bowl showcases their love for midcentury modern housewares; and images of a coffee carafe, a bike, and garden vegetables inform people of their everyday interests. On display in each of their homes, the crest is a testament to their creativity, friendship, and living arrangement.

Two-Family Crest

Inspired by their newly purchased duplex, their neighborhood, and their common interests, best friends Chika Eustace and Jean Lee crafted a family crest from wood. A family crest is a good way to graphically represent your interests and values. If you are new to working with wood, they suggest using a soft wood like pine or asking a professional to cut the wood forms.

Finished size as shown: 14 x 13"

MATERIALS

12 x 24" piece ¾"-thick pine wood with a consistent grain and few knots

Two 3 x 6" pieces 1"-thick walnut wood

Wood glue

16-ounce can spray-on clear coat

Sawtooth hanger

Nail

TOOLS

Copier

Laser copier

Double-stick tape

Pencil (optional)

60- to 150-grit sandpaper

Tack cloth

Painter's tape

Wood-burning tool kit with a selection of interchangeable tips, including a transfer tip and a fine-point tip

2 medium clamps and 4 small clamps

Utility knife

Goggles

Dust mask

Jigsaw or band saw with a thin blade

Table saw or miter box with a handsaw

Electric fan

Scrap wood

Pliers

Cloth or rag

Cardboard

Hammer

1. From the forms on page 156, choose a house design to go with your shield to make the base of your family crest. Photocopy these images, enlarging them by 300% (size will be approximately 8 ½ x 13"). If you wish to include them, photocopy the ribbon or arugula shapes as well, enlarging them by 300%.

2. Choose icons from page 157 that fit your theme. Photocopy the images, resizing them if necessary, and place them on the photocopied shield or ribbon, rearranging until you are satisfied with the composition. Use double-stick tape to attach the images. Keep the ribbon composition separate from the shield. You can also draw your own images if none of those provided appeal to you. Letters and numbers can be included by drawing them freehand or using a computer to print them on paper. Remember that if you use text or make your own illustrations on paper, they need to be drawn in reverse for the image transfer process. Also, leave enough material around the final form so you can clamp the wood to a work surface.

Another option is to trace the form of the house and shield directly onto the wood with a pencil and draw your

⟫⟶

Chika peels back a corner of the paper to check her transfer progress (Step 5).

symbols and images freehand on it. If you do so, sand the front surface of your wood and wipe with a tack cloth before drawing. If you choose this option, you can skip Steps 3 to 6.

3. Photocopy the final composition of your shield, ribbon, and any additional shapes using a laser copier for the heat transfer process. Set aside.

4. Choose one side of the wood to be the front of your family crest. Sand the front surface and wipe with a tack cloth. Starting with the shield composition, use painter's tape to tape the corners of the laser-copied image face down on the wood. When you place the image on the wood, make sure there is enough material around the form to clamp to a work surface.

5. Using the transfer tip on your wood-burning tool, apply heat to the back of your image until the toner from the copy transfers to the wood. Slowly peel back a corner of the paper to peek under and check your transfer progress. Be careful not to move the paper while it is transferring or you will compromise the clarity of your traced image.

6. Repeat Steps 4 and 5 for any additional shapes, including the ribbon.

7. Clamp the wood with the transferred or hand-drawn image to a stable surface using the medium clamps. With a utility knife, trace the outline of each shape you will cut out.

8. Wearing goggles and a dust mask, cut out the shapes with a jigsaw. If your shapes are complex, they may require multiple approaches with the saw and "nibbling" at the wood in tight corners. Reposition your piece as you cut so that you always have a comfortable approach, good visibility with the blade, and enough clearance for the saw.

9. Using either a table saw or miter box and handsaw, cut the pieces of walnut wood on one edge at a mitered angle to match the angle at the center top of the house and shield. This will form the roof.

10. With sandpaper, smooth the edges of your cut shapes and wipe the excess sawdust with a tack cloth.

11. On a work surface in a well-ventilated area, turn on your wood-burning tool. Place an electric fan in front of you so that it blows any smoke created by the wood burning out through a nearby window. With a fine-point tool tip, press into the wood to capture small details in the design elements. Use the larger chisel-shaped tips to burn larger areas. Practice on a piece of scrap wood to get comfortable with the textures and lines you can create with the tool. If your tool tip becomes loose, use a pair of pliers to tighten it. Keep a damp cloth handy to wipe the tip of your wood-burning tool as you use it. If you make any mistakes, sand the marks to remove or dull them.

12. Apply wood glue to the top of the house shape and to the ribbon pieces. Clamp the walnut wood to the top of the house and the ribbon pieces to the shield with the small clamps. Avoid making clamp marks on your piece by placing a thin piece of cardboard between the clamp and the wood surface. Allow the glue to dry. Remove clamps and cardboard.

13. Apply spray-on clear coat to protect the wood from stains and dust.

14. Attach a sawtooth hanger to the back of your crest. Hammer a nail into the wall and hang the crest.

Jean sands a wood piece (Step 10), while Chika burns the design onto the wood using the wood-burning tool (Step 11).

Modern Norens

joanna mendicino
san mateo, california

As a teen, Joanna Mendicino had modest room

decor needs: she simply wanted a door she could close for privacy. However, her mother, Ritsuko Spalding, wasn't too keen on bending their home's open-door rule, so she offered Joanna a compromise: Japanese noren curtains in her doorway. Indeed, norens, typically two-panel curtains that cover the top half of the doorway opening, were not new to Joanna. Although she was born in North Carolina and grew up in cities throughout the United States, one of her father's military assignments afforded her the opportunity to live in her mother's home country, Japan, from age five to seven. Joanna fondly remembered seeing norens decorated with kanji characters (Chinese characters used in the Japanese writing system) at the entrances to businesses, primarily restaurants. Joanna was pleased that the norens obscured complete visual access to her room, providing her with the sense of privacy she so fiercely desired. For her mother, it also became a way to bring more of her Japanese culture into her home.

Fast-forward to age thirty-two, and Joanna is now a ceramic artist. In her work, the influence of Japanese sensibilities is evident, especially through the ceramic forms of exaggerated, round animalia. Likewise, Joanna is looking at her Japanese heritage for inspiration as she decorates her first home. Recalling both the utility and the decorative potential of norens, Joanna found herself turning once again to her mother for these curtains. The norens Joanna had as a teenager were store-bought and had traditional Japanese imagery. This time, she asked her mother to teach her to sew them. Naturally, this excited her mother, an avid sewer, who had been trying to convince Joanna to get behind a sewing machine for years. Because norens carry both nostalgia and Japanese culture, it was fitting that they become their first sewing project together. Joanna's idea to customize her norens gave her the opportunity to express her current sensibilities as a designer. Carving out illustrations on a rubber stamp pad, she presents her own patterns and modern motifs inspired by Japanese pop graphics on this traditional Japanese decorative curtain.

Modern Norens

Connecting with her Japanese heritage, Joanna Mendicino designed and sewed noren curtains for her home. The instructions for these doorway curtains are for a standard 36"-wide opening. If your doorway is a different width, measure the width, add 4 inches, and divide that number by 2 to get the final width you'll need for each panel. Depending on how much privacy you want, you can increase the length of the curtains as well.

Finished size as shown: Each panel is 18" wide by 30" long for total width of 36"

MATERIALS

2 yards medium-weight pure cotton or cotton-blend fabric

Matching sewing thread

6 x 12" rubber stamp carving block (or use a premade rubber stamp)

Screen-printing ink for fabric

Tension curtain rod

TOOLS

Clear acrylic grid ruler

Fabric marker

Fabric scissors

Sewing pins

Sewing machine

Iron and ironing board

Utility knife

Fine-point permanent marker

Lino cutter

½"-wide paintbrush

1. With a clear grid ruler, fabric marker, and fabric scissors, measure, mark, and cut two panels of fabric 20" wide by 33½" long. (If you want norens of a different length, add 3½" to your desired length for each panel to account for the channel at the top that the curtain rod will slide through, as well as the double folded hem at the bottom of each panel.)

2. Place one panel on top of the other with the right sides together. Match all four corners of the two panels and pin together along the right side. With a fabric marker and ruler, measure and mark 11" from the top of the right side. With your sewing machine and matching thread, sew a 1" seam allowance down the right side to the 11" mark, backstitching at the end. Remove the pins.

3. Unfold the panels and lay them flat on your ironing board with the wrong sides facing up. Using an iron, press the seam allowances open. At the end of the seam, press 1" to the wrong side along the remaining length of the panels at the center front.

4. Starting with the right panel, measure 1" from the outer edge. Fold to the wrong side at the 1" mark and press with an iron. Repeat for the left panel and the bottom of each panel.

$\gg\!\!\longrightarrow$

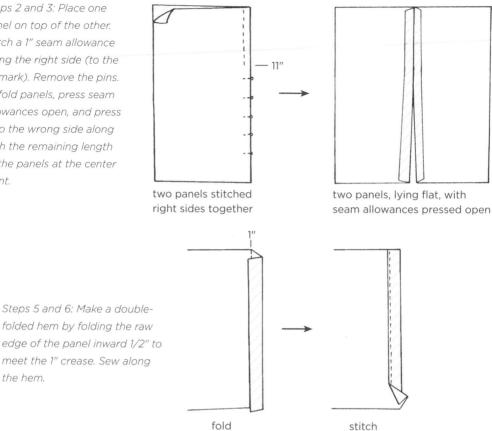

Steps 2 and 3: Place one panel on top of the other. Stitch a 1" seam allowance along the right side (to the 11" mark). Remove the pins. Unfold panels, press seam allowances open, and press 1" to the wrong side along with the remaining length of the panels at the center front.

two panels stitched right sides together

two panels, lying flat, with seam allowances pressed open

Steps 5 and 6: Make a double-folded hem by folding the raw edge of the panel inward 1/2" to meet the 1" crease. Sew along the hem.

fold

stitch

5. To make a double-folded hem, start with the outer edge of the right panel, open the fold, and fold the raw edge of the panel inward ½" to meet the 1" crease. Press the edge with an iron. Refold on the original fold line. Pin along the edge.

6. Using your sewing machine, stitch along the inner fold, backstitching at the ends. Remove the pins.

7. Repeat steps 5 and 6 at the center of the two panels, on the outer edge of the left panel, and the bottom of each panel.

8. To create the channel at the top, fold the edge of the panel 2½" to the wrong side and press. Next, open the fold, and fold the raw edge inward ½". Press the edge with an iron. Fold along the

2½" line again, pin the ½" fold to the panel, and stitch along the inner fold, backstitching at the ends. Remove the pins.

9. Place your finished noren face up on a work surface.

10. With a utility knife, cut a 4" square from your rubber stamp block.

11. With your permanent marker, draw a design onto the block. Designate positive space (the part of the image that will appear when you stamp) by coloring or putting hash marks within the lines. Negative space will be the part of the image recessed on the stamp. Using the lino cutter, remove the negative space. Make sure you cut deep enough, so that the ink will only appear on the positive space, but not so deep that the blade tears the surface.

12. Using a paintbrush, apply an even layer of screen-printing ink to the raised surface of your stamp. Test the stamp on a scrap piece of fabric before stamping on your noren. Make sure you press down firmly on the stamp, holding for a couple of seconds to ensure the design transfers completely. If the image is too light, you will either need to thicken your ink layer or add more pressure when stamping. When you are comfortable with stamping, stamp the noren panels in any fashion that you find visually pleasing. You can use the design simply as a border or you can cover the entire noren.

13. Once the fabric is dry, iron it on high heat to set the ink.

14. Slide the tension curtain rod through the top channel and hang at the top of the doorway.

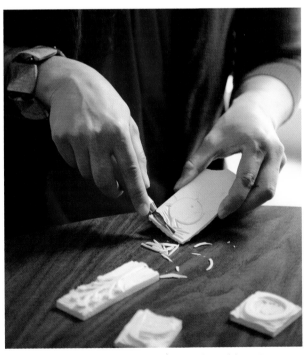

Joanna carves a design freehand into the rubber stamp block. She uses a lino cutter to remove the negative space (Step 11).

Jewelry Tree

carolina saxl
napa, california

Even though Carolina Saxl had been away from home for more than nine years, living in places like Chicago, Charleston, and the San Francisco Bay Area, she had always dreamt of returning to her hometown of Newton, Kansas, for her wedding. Newton is an idyllic, tight-knit community where her grandparents, parents, and many relatives still reside. When she got engaged to Chris Saxl, he agreed to wed in Kansas.

But picking the location was child's play compared to the minutiae that ensued in the months leading up to the big day. A jewelry designer and crafter, Carolina was intent on making their wedding a DIY family affair. With a you-can-wear-it-again (or rather you-can-use-it-again) sensibility, Carolina wanted to create a centerpiece that was meaningful but could also double as home décor. The end result: a manzanita branch centerpiece that can also be used as a decorative jewelry stand.

Two weeks before the wedding, Carolina enlisted her parents to help with the centerpieces. First, she asked her father, Charles Graber, a surgeon by profession but a woodworker in his off-duty hours, to cut tree trunks to make the wood bases. This was not the first time Carolina and her father had done a woodworking project together. In fact, Charles had put his daughter behind a table saw at the age of twelve and, over the years, she had assisted him on projects such as wooden sailboats and stools. Her mother, Margret, an avid quilter, naturally was asked to sew the stuffed birds that would sit atop the branches. Likewise, she and her mother had sewn many projects together while she was growing up, including doll's clothing, pillows, and quilts.

In the end, Carolina and Chris had a centerpiece with several layers of meaning. The manzanita branches from California symbolize Carolina and Chris's new home base. The birds recall her mother's passion for sewing. The wood foundation, cut from the Osage orange trees on Carolina's grandmother's farm, literally represents a piece of Kansas as well as her father's woodworking skills. A souvenir from their wedding, the centerpiece now has a second life sitting atop their dresser displaying jewelry of Carolina's design.

Jewelry Tree

Carolina Saxl assembled this wedding centerpiece-cum-jewelry tree from a manzanita tree branch and wood from her grandmother's farm. Manzanita is the best decorative branch, but mitsumata branches are an alternative. Look for a piece with lots of small branches, especially ones that extend outward and are strong enough for hanging jewelry.

Finished size as shown:
18" high, 8" diameter at base

MATERIALS

Wood round with bark or slice of a tree stump or branch (8" to 9" diameter, 3" to 4" high)

9 x 12" piece brown wool felt

Manzanita tree branch, 12" to 16" tall

Wood glue

3-ounce package reindeer moss

TOOLS

Permanent marker

Fabric scissors

Glue gun and glue sticks

Electric drill with drill bits

Scrap plywood

1. On your work surface, place your wood round on top of your sheet of felt. With a permanent marker, trace around the base of the wood round. Remove the wood round and, with fabric scissors, cut the outlined area from the felt. Using a glue gun, glue the felt to the base of the wood round. This will prevent the wood from scratching the surface that it rests on. Set aside.

2. Select a drill bit that is slightly wider than your branch and place it in your electric drill. Drill a series of at least five holes of varying depths and angles in the plywood scrap. This test will ensure that your branch will sit securely in place and allow you to play with the desired height and direction of your branch. Test your branch in each hole to see which one looks most pleasing.

3. With a permanent marker, mark the center of your wood round. Drill a hole on this mark according to the depth and direction determined by the test plywood. Place your branch in the hole and modify the hole, if needed.

4. Covering only the surface that will be going into the wood base, apply a generous layer of wood glue over the end of the branch. Place the end of the branch into the hole and adjust until you get the proper angle. Apply more glue, if necessary. (Note: It's okay for excess glue to come out of the hole because the entire surface will be covered with moss.) Allow the glue to dry completely.

5. Apply glue with your glue gun to a small section on top of the base. Place the moss atop the warm glue and press down gently. Continue until the entire base is covered. To keep your moss alive, spray with water every two weeks.

Wallpaper Luminarias

christiana coop & aimee lagos
minneapolis, minnesota

With a friendship spanning more than two
decades, Christiana Coop and Aimee Lagos like to reminisce about their
childhood summers spent hanging out at the local swimming pool, time apart
during college, pursuing law degrees, jointly starting a wallpaper business,
and more recently, launching an online retail store, Hygge & West, together.
Despite all the memories they share, nothing strikes a nostalgic chord quite
like the winters they spent as children in their hometown of Los Alamos, New
Mexico. The glowing thread across all those winters: luminarias.

At its simplest, a luminaria is a decorated paper bag filled with sand and
a candle. A New Mexico tradition, it is used to decorate driveways and front
lawns during the holidays. Originally a spiritual symbol (luminaria means
"little torch" and was used to welcome the Christ child into one's home), it has
developed into more of a cultural tradition in an area where Spanish, Native
American, and American cultures meet.

Christiana and Aimee vividly recall the times they spent making luminarias together at each other's homes and at school. But their strongest memories
are of the luminaria-decorated homes in the Barranca Mesa neighborhood of
Los Alamos. In the week leading up to Christmas Day, Christiana and Aimee
would become tourists in their hometown, taking a slow drive with their parents through the main artery of the subdivision. They welcomed the requisite
traffic jam, because it allowed them to ogle house after house radiating with
festive lights. They remember their astonishment at how people were able to
light so many luminarias and place them in extraordinary locations throughout the facades of their homes and even along the rooflines.

Luminarias are meant to be temporary décor. But Christiana and Aimee,
now residing in Minneapolis, wanted to create a more permanent reminder of
their hometown. Using glass vases decorated with wallpaper instead of paper
bags, they've fashioned contemporary luminarias that meld their present interests with their childhoods past.

Wallpaper Luminarias

Christiana Coop and Aimee Lagos bring back their childhood pastime with luminarias made from glass and wallpaper. Though they use wallpaper, you can use any heavy decorative paper. The soft glow from the luminarias is a nice way to bring ambient light into a room.

Finished sizes as shown:
4 x 3 x 6" and 4 x 3 x 9"

MATERIALS

Wallpaper scraps or craft paper (see Note)

Rectangular glass vase

Candle

TOOLS

Soft lead pencil

Straightedge

Small utility knife

Cutting mat

Handheld craft punch

Hollow hole punch

Craft hammer

Double-stick tape

Note: The project shown was made with Hygge & West wallpaper. Alternatively, you could use any wallpaper or other decorative paper of similar weight.

1. Lay the wallpaper face down on your work surface. Place the vase on the wallpaper. Loosely wrap the wallpaper around the sides of the vase to ensure complete coverage. Unwrap the wallpaper and smooth it out with your hand.

2. Using a soft lead pencil, trace a line on the wallpaper along the top and bottom edges of the vase; set the vase aside. Using a straightedge, extend those lines toward each edge of the wallpaper. Again wrap the wallpaper around the vase and, with your pencil, mark where the two edges meet. To be safe, leave a little extra paper for an overlap. Lay the paper flat again, and with your straightedge, extend the meeting line from top to bottom so that it crosses the two previous lines you drew.

3. Using a small utility knife, a cutting mat, and a straightedge, cut along the drawn lines. Wrap the trimmed wallpaper around your vase to ensure that all edges are flush. Make creases along the corners so you know where each face of the vase lines up on the wallpaper. Set the vase aside.

4. With your handheld craft punch, add decorative holes to the top and bottom edges of the wallpaper. To put holes in the middle of the wallpaper, use a hollow hole punch and a craft hammer, making sure to place a cutting mat beneath the wallpaper.

5. Apply double-stick tape along all the edges on the back of the wallpaper. Wrap the wallpaper around the vase, and press lightly so the wallpaper adheres to the glass.

6. Place a candle inside the vase.

Family Teepee

billie lopez & tootie maldonado
los angeles, california

On any given weekend, you'll likely find Billie

Lopez and Tootie Maldonado hiking, picnicking, kayaking, playing beach volleyball, camping, or engaging in some other outdoor activity. These two best friends, and now co-owners of the Los Angeles boutique ReForm School, have known each other since they attended El Rancho High School in Pico Rivera, California. Back then they were just acquaintances. It wasn't until later that they grew closer, realizing they had more in common than just attending the same school—namely, a love for craft and the outdoors.

Although they didn't grow up together, Billie and Tootie both have fond memories of being engaged with nature through camping or spending time indoors learning a craft. Billie would go camping with her parents, brothers, and sisters at least once every summer, often frequenting campsites along different California rivers, such as the Kern River. Likewise, Tootie grew up doing large multifamily camping trips in Ojai with aunts, uncles, and cousins. Staying indoors for both girls meant creating crafts such as latch hook rugs, friendship bracelets, and clothes for their Barbies. Tootie also learned to sew and crochet from her grandmother. "It was my grandmother's way of quieting us down while she watched her novellas," Tootie laughs.

Nowadays, Billie and Tootie consider each other family. Billie, her husband, Adan, and daughters, Emma, Frankie, and Tallulah, along with Tootie, her son, Adam, and her boyfriend, Brad, often do outdoor activities together. In fact, they took Emma on her first camping trip when she was only six weeks old. With a vintage quilt top, cotton fabric, recycled fabric rope, and vintage buttons, Billie, Tootie, and Billie's daughters have put together a teepee project that embodies their dual love for nature and craft. It also provides a way for Billie's girls to enjoy the outdoors in their backyard throughout the year.

Family Teepee

Billie Lopez and Tootie Maldonado pronounce their love for the outdoors with their family teepee made from a vintage quilt top and bamboo poles. If you don't have a quilt top suitable for this purpose, try looking for one at local thrift stores or consider sewing one yourself from your family's clothing (see Dad's Patchwork Coverlet on page 26). Alternatively, you can use an old or new flat sheet.

Finished size as shown: 88 x 52"

MATERIALS

Old quilt top or flat sheet (preferably queen or king size)

10 yards cotton fabric

1 ⅞ yards patterned cotton fabric (entrance trim)

⅜ yard patterned cotton fabric (hem facing)

Vintage napkin or handkerchief

27 x 80 ½" piece butcher paper

Two 2"-square pieces fusible interfacing

Matching sewing thread

2 pieces ⅜"-wide elastic, each 6" long

Three 3'-long pieces of rope

Three 1" buttons

Straight twig 2" longer than your napkin or handkerchief

3' jute twine

Six 8'-long bamboo poles

TOOLS

Iron and ironing board

Yardstick or clear acrylic grid ruler

Paper scissors

Pencil

Straight pins

Fabric marker

Fabric scissors

Sewing machine

Hand-sewing needle

Large safety pin

Paint pens in assorted colors

Stepstool or ladder

Sewing the Teepee Cover

1. Wash, dry, and iron all the fabric before cutting.

2. On a large work surface, orient your butcher paper vertically. Draw a parallel line 1 ½" from the top edge. Fold the paper along this line. The folded portion of the paper will become the pattern for the casing, or drawstring channel, at the top of the teepee.

>>—→

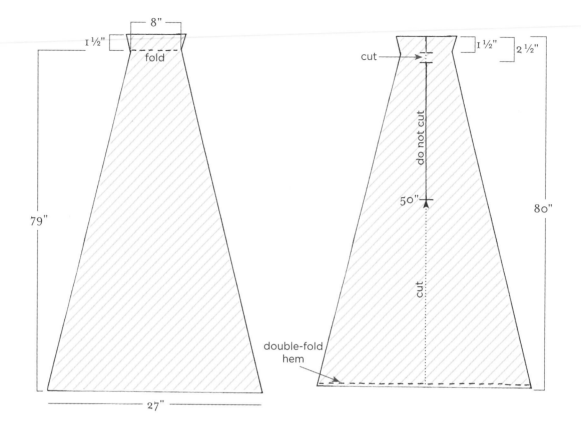

Steps 2 and 3: Single teepee panel template.

Steps 6, 7, and 9: Entrance panel template.

3. Using the template and dimensions above as a guideline, outline the pattern of one teepee panel on the butcher paper. Your pattern should be 8" wide at the top along the fold line, 79" long from the fold line to base, and 27" wide at the base. Cut out the pattern with paper scissors, cutting through both layers of paper at the top.

4. Unfold the teepee pattern at the top and place it on the right side of the quilt top, positioning the wide base of the pattern in one corner of the quilt top. Pin the pattern in place. Trace around the pattern with the fabric marker, using a ruler to mark the straight edges. Remove the pattern,

pin to a new area of the quilt top, and trace again. Repeat to trace a total of three teepee panels onto the quilt top. Cut out the teepee panels on the marked lines using fabric scissors. Set aside.

5. Fold the solid fabric in half crosswise, wrong sides together. Unfold the teepee pattern at the top and pin the pattern to the cotton fabric. Cut around the pattern with fabric scissors to make two teepee panels. Remove the pattern. Repeat 2 more times to cut a total of 6 cotton teepee panels.

6. To make the entrance panel to your teepee, place one solid panel, wrong side up, on the ironing board. Fold over and press ¼" to the wrong side along the 27"-wide base. Fold over ¼" again to make a narrow double-fold hem. Stitch close to the first fold.

7. Fold the entrance panel in half lengthwise, wrong sides together and press a crease along the fold line. Open the panel, wrong side up. Using a fabric marker and ruler along the crease line, measure and mark 1 ½" and 2 ½" from the top edge of the panel (this marks the opening in the drawstring channel) and 50" from the bottom of the panel (this marks the top of the entrance opening).

8. Following the manufacturer's instructions, fuse a 2" square of fusible interfacing to the wrong side of the entrance panel, centered over the marks at the top (this reinforces the drawstring opening). Center and fuse the remaining 2" square of fusible interfacing over the mark 50" from the bottom of the panel (this reinforces the top of the entrance opening).

9. Using fabric scissors, make two cuts along the crease line of the entrance panel starting at the mark 1 ½" from the top edge of the panel to the 2 ½" mark and starting from the bottom of the panel to the 50" mark.

10. Cut two strips, each measuring 51" long by 4" wide, from the patterned fabric. With the wrong sides of the strips facing up, fold over and press ½" to the wrong side on each of the long edges. Then fold over and press ½" to the wrong side on the short ends of the strips. Fold each strip in half lengthwise and press.

11. Place the teepee entrance panel, right side up, on the work surface. Place one patterned fabric strip, right side out, around one side of the teepee opening. The edge of the teepee fabric should sit in the center fold of the patterned fabric strip; the bottom edge of the strip should align with the bottom edge of the teepee entrance panel. Pin in place. Repeat for the other side of the teepee opening.

12. Fold each piece of elastic in half. Pin the ends of one elastic strip underneath the front left edge of the patterned fabric trim, 28" from the bottom edge of the

⟫⟶

teepee, to create a loop. Repeat with the remaining piece of elastic on the right side of the teepee opening. These loops will act as tiebacks to keep the teepee entrance open.

13. On the front of the teepee opening, stitch ⅛" from the pinned edges of the patterned fabric on each side of the entrance panel, backstitching at the ends and across the encased ends of the elastic strips. For extra security, hand stitch the patterned entrance trim together at the center top for about 1". Set the entrance panel aside.

14. To line your quilt panels, pin one quilt top panel to a solid panel, wrong sides together, along the long edges. Stitch along the pinned edges, using a ⅝" seam allowance. Repeat with the two remaining quilt top panels and two solid panels.

15. Pin the quilt side of one quilt panel to a new solid panel, right sides together, along one long edge. Stitch ¾" from the edge, backstitching at the ends. Press the seam allowances toward the lining of the quilt panel. Repeat to join the next quilt top panel to the remaining long edge of the previous solid panel. Continue the alternating pattern, joining the last quilt top panel to the entrance panel, and allowing the quilt top panel to extend ½" beyond the lower edge of the entrance panel. Join the remaining side of the entrance panel to the remaining side of the first quilt panel in the same manner. Press all seam allowances toward the lining of the quilt panel sections.

16. Trim the bottom two seam allowances on the long seams of the quilt panel sections to ⅜". Press under ¼" on the remaining seam allowances and pin to the lining side of the quilt panel. Edgestitch along the folds through all layers to encase raw edges.

17. For the hem facing, cut a 3 x 129" strip from the patterned fabric, piecing as necessary for length. Fold the strip in half lengthwise and press. Pin the long raw edge of the strip to the lower edge of the teepee, right sides together, except along the hem of the entrance panel. Stitch ½" from the raw edges. Trim the seam allowances to ¼" wide. Press the band toward the inside of the teepee. Turn

View of the teepee top from the interior shows how the alternating lined quilt panels and solid panels connect.

Elastic loop sewn beneath the entrance trim acts as a tieback when hooked to the button, keeping the teepee open (Step 20).

the short ends under and hand-stitch to the seam allowances along the entrance panel. Hand tack the upper edge of the band to the seam allowances between the teepee panels.

18. Turn the teepee cover inside out, fold the top edge ½" to the wrong side and press. Fold the top edge over 1", press, and pin along the fold. Stitch along the first fold to make the drawstring channel, backstitching at the end. Turn the teepee right side out.

19. Affix a large safety pin to the end of a 3' length of rope. Insert the rope into the opening in the drawstring channel at the center front, pull the rope through the channel, and pull the end back out through the center front opening. Remove the safety pin and knot each end of the rope.

20. With your finger, draw a line from the elastic loop along the entrance trim, outward across the entrance panel until it meets the seam joining the entrance panel to the quilt top fabric. Hand-stitch a button on this spot. Repeat for the opposite side. Insert the buttons into the elastic loops to keep the teepee entrance open.

21. Hand-stitch the last button centered 8" above the top of the teepee's entrance, to hang the sign. Set the teepee cover aside.

≫⟶

Step 25: Tie the bamboo poles together using clove hitch knots.

A

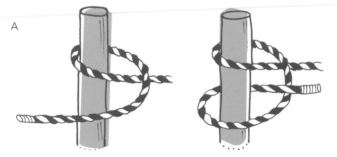

For the first pole, create a clove hitch knot starting with the end of the rope.

B

Pull both rope ends in opposite directions to tighen the knot.

C

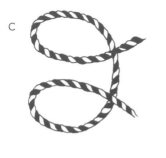

Continue making knots on the other poles, tightening the knots as shown in Step B.

Making the Sign

22. With a fabric marker, lightly mark a message (e.g., "Keep Out") on the napkin or handkerchief using very simple hand lettering. Using a sewing machine, stitch over the writing going forward and backward several times to create thick lines and a sketchy look. This will be the sign hung in front of the teepee's opening.

23. Align the top of the cloth sign with your twig, centering it. Pinching a top corner of the sign, knot and wrap one piece of twine around the corner of the sign and the twig. Leave about a 12" slack on the twine and knot and wrap the other corner of the sign. Trim the excess twine. Set aside.

Decorating and Assembling the Teepee

24. On the bamboo poles, use paint pens to create fun markings, such as arrows or stripes. Allow the paint to dry.

25. Lay the poles on the ground. Tie them together with one of the 3' ropes, using clove hitch knots (see illustration above) and leaving approximately 1" of space between each knot/pole. There will be 6 knots, 1 on each pole. Form your knots approximately 10" down from the top of the poles. Tie the remaining length of rope together tightly using whatever knot you wish as long as it's secure.

26. Bring the poles to an erect position with the knotted ends pointing upward. Imagining there is a clock on the ground, place the ends of the poles in the 1, 3, 5, 7, 9, and 11 o'clock positions. (You may need two sets of hands for this step.) Leave a slightly larger gap between the bottoms of the poles at the 5 and 7 o'clock spots for the teepee's opening. At this point it may be helpful to mark numbers on the poles to help you set them up more quickly next time.

27. Using a stepstool or ladder, place the teepee cover over the frame, allowing the bottom edge to touch the ground. Tighten the drawstring around the top of the cover. Wrap and tie a second piece of rope around the top of the teepee just under the drawstring. Hang your cloth sign on the button above the teepee's entrance.

Tootie and Billie arrange the teepee poles in the 1, 3, 5, 7, 9, and 11 o'clock positions (Step 26).

Appendix

ALPONA PILLOW ARTWORK

Oorbee Roy's alpona art, a type of Indian folk art, is shown below. Enlarge the artwork by 300% to create the stencil used to design the fabric on the 16 x 16" pillow shown on page 62.

Note: The copyright to the image above belongs to Oorbee Roy. The image cannot be reproduced for commercial use. Please use image for personal use only.

FOLKLORE CHAIR DRAWING

Diana Fayt drew the roses and roosters pattern (shown below) as an expression of her Hungarian roots. Enlarge the artwork by 290% to screen-print this pattern onto fabric to cover a chair cushion. The project can be found on page 102.

Note: The copyright to the image above belongs to Diana Fayt. The image cannot be reproduced for commercial use. Please use image for personal use only.

LETTERS AND NUMBERS FOR NEEDLEPOINT RACQUETS

Use the charted letters and numbers below to help you draft your needlepoint design on graph paper. You can include your initials or a special date just as Amy Holbrook did for her needlepoint racquets on page 108.

Note: The copyright to the images above belongs to AMH Design LLC. The images cannot be reproduced for commercial use. Please use images for personal use only.

CITYSCAPE COLLAGE ICONS

Lorena Siminovich layered paper cut from these building and transportation icons to portray a cityscape shown on page 114. Feel free to modify the sizes of these icons to fit your collage.

Note: The copyright to the images above belongs to Lorena Siminovich. The images cannot be reproduced for commercial use. Please use images for personal use only.

TWO-FAMILY CREST FORMS

Chika Eustace and Jean Lee created a 14 x 13" two-family crest on wood (see page 122). Choose a house design to go with your shield form for the base. The ribbon and the arugula leaves can also be added to your design. Enlarge all pieces by 300% to make a 14"-wide crest.

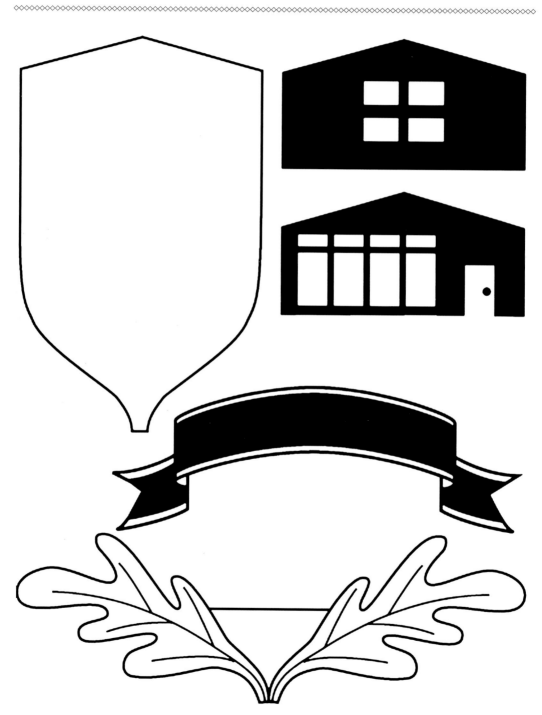

TWO-FAMILY CREST ICONS

To express your interests on your crest, use the icons below or others of your choosing to decorate your wood surface. Modify the sizes as needed using a copier or a scanner and computer.

Note: The copyright to the images on pages 156–157 belong to Chika Eustace and Jean Lee. The images cannot be reproduced for commercial use. Please use images for personal use only.

Resource Guide

CONTRIBUTORS

To learn more about the contributors featured in this book, please visit their websites:

Cathy Callahan, Cathy of California, www.cathyofcalifornia.com

Joy Deangdeelert Cho, Oh Joy!, www.ohjoy.com

Lisa Congdon, Lisa Congdon Art + Illustration, www.lisacongdon.com

Susan Connor, SusyJack*, www.susyjack.com

Christiana Coop, Hygge & West, www.hyggeandwestshop.com

Anna Corpron & Sean Auyeung, Sub-Studio Design, www.sub-studio.com

Brooke Davies, Clothpony, www.clothpony.com

Rae Dunn, Rae Dunn, www.raedunn.com

Chika Eustace, Chikabird, www.chikabird.350.com

Diana Fayt, Diana Fayt, www.dianafayt.com

Samantha Hahn, Samantha Hahn, www.samanthahahn.com

Amy Holbrook, AMH Design, www.amhdesignonline.com

Meg Mateo Ilasco, Mateo Ilasco, www.mateoilasco.com

Lisa Wong Jackson, Good On Paper Design, www.goodonpaperdesign.com

Sian Keegan, Sian Keegan, www.siankeegan.com

Aimee Lagos, Hygge & West, www.hyggeandwestshop.com

Anh-Minh Le, Anh-Minh.com, www.anh-minh.com

Jean Lee, Ladies & Gentlemen, www.ladiesandgentlemenstudio.com

Billie Lopez & Tootie Maldonado, ReForm School, www.reformschoolrules.com

Haile McCollum, Fontaine Maury, www.fontainemaury.com

Joanna Mendicino, J. Mendicino, www.jmendicino.com

Oorbee Roy, OM Home, www.omhome.com

Carolina Saxl, Carrie Saxl, www.carriesaxl.com

Christine Schmidt, Yellow Owl Workshop, www.yellowowlworkshop.com

Lorena Siminovich, Petit Collage, www.petitcollage.com

Paula Smail, Henry Road, www.henryroad.com

Lauren Smith & Derek Fagerstrom, The Curiosity Shoppe, www.curiosityshoppeonline.com

SOURCES FOR SUPPLIES

Most of the materials and supplies used to make the projects in this book can be found at art supply and hardware retailers nationwide. If you cannot find a specific item, try these online resources:

Acrylic

TAP Plastics, www.tapplastics.com

Atlases

Maps.com, www.maps.com

Bamboo Poles

Bamboo Expressions, www.bambooexpressions.com

Cotton Piping Cord

Create for Less, www.createforless.com

Fabric and Notions

Fabric Temptations, www.fabrictemptations.com
Jo-Ann Fabrics and Crafts, www.joann.com
Mood Fabrics, www.moodfabrics.com
Purl Patchwork, www.purlsoho.com
Reprodepot Fabrics, www.reprodepot.com

General Craft

Dick Blick Art Materials, www.dickblick.com
Michaels, www.michaels.com
Pearl, www.pearlpaint.com
Save-on-crafts, www.save-on-crafts.com

Manzanita Branches and Reindeer Moss

Blooms & Branches, www.bloomsandbranches.com
Nettleton Hollow, www.nettletonhollow.com

Mold-Making

Ace Hardware, www.acehardware.com
Smooth-On, www.smooth-on.com
TAP Plastics, www.tapplastics.com

Needlepoint

A.C. Moore Arts & Crafts, www.acmoore.com
A to Z Needlepoint, www.a-z-needlepoint.com
Crafter's Market, www.craftersmarket.net

Rope

Knot & Rope Supply, www.knotandrope.com

Test Tubes

Lake Charles Manufacturing, www.testtubesonline.com

Wallpaper

Ferm Living, www.fermlivingshop.us
Hygge & West, www.hyggeandwestshop.com
The Internet Wallpaper Store, www.wallpaperstore.com
Walnut Wallpaper, www.walnutwallpaper.com

Woodworking

Dunn Lumber, www.dunnlumber.com
The Home Depot, www.homedepot.com
Rockler, www.rockler.com

Acknowledgments

Foremost, I would like to thank my editor, Melanie Falick, for taking my book proposal and making it better. Thank you for your enthusiasm, encouragement, and patience. Working with you on this project has been an absolute joy.

Thanks also to editors Liana Allday, Karen Levy, Dawn Anderson, and Karen Manthey for their attention to detail and for helping me to form the right words, especially when it came to explaining processes and techniques.

My gratitude goes to my agent, Lilly Ghahremani, for believing in this project and finding the perfect home for it.

Thank you to everyone who contributed their wonderful, personal projects to this book. A special thank you goes to Cathy Callahan, Paula Smail, Amy Holbrook, Samantha Hahn, Lisa Congdon, Christiana Coop, Lisa Wong Jackson, Lauren Smith, Derek Fagerstrom, Lorena Siminovich, and Rae Dunn for allowing us into your beautiful homes for the photo shoots.

I couldn't have made this book without the help of my two assistants, Virginia Dolen and Kimberly Kulka. Thank you, Virginia, for your help with proofreading as well as for managing the giant matrix of scheduling, organizing, and contacting the contributors; and thank you, Kim, for handling all the ongoing studio business so that I could work on this book.

My gratitude goes to photographer Thayer Allyson Gowdy, whose talent is only exceeded by her exuberant personality. I thank you and your assistant, Brian Stevens, for working your magic on every shoot and making the projects and participants look their absolute best.

Also, thank you to my styling helpers, Marvin Ilasco, Kimberly Kulka, and Virginia Dolen, for your discerning eye and muscle power, not to mention your dry humor and sharp wit that made every shoot a fun experience.

Thank you to my good friends Pamela Park Kawada and Naoya and Jennifer Imanishi for housing me during the Los Angeles shoot.

To my parents, Alfonso and Dely Mateo, for instilling an appreciation for my heritage and culture and for allowing me to dig through the attic for Filipino pieces to put in my home. Finally, to my husband, Marvin Ilasco, and our kids, Lauryn and Miles, thank you for your wonderful encouragement, support, and enthusiasm, and for letting me stay glued to my laptop to finish this book.

Meg Mateo Ilasco is a designer, writer, and illustrator. She is the principal of Mateo Ilasco, a design studio in the San Francisco Bay Area that creates paper and home goods. She is the author of *Craft, Inc.; Craft, Inc. Business Planner; Creative, Inc;* and *The Space Planner: A Home Decorating and Design Workbook.* Visit her website at www.mateoilasco.com.